T0321397

THE LILAC TREE

A RABBI'S REFLECTIONS ON LOVE, COURAGE, AND HISTORY

AMMIEL HIRSCH

WICKED SON

A WICKED SON BOOK
An Imprint of Post Hill Press
ISBN: 978-1-63758-746-1
ISBN (eBook): 978-1-63758-747-8

The Lilac Tree:
A Rabbi's Reflections on Love, Courage, and History
© 2023 by Rabbi Ammiel Hirsch
All Rights Reserved

Cover Design by Tiffani Shea

Post Hill Press
New York • Nashville
WickedSonBooks.com

Published in the United States of America
1 2 3 4 5 6 7 8 9 10

To Olga:
A woman like this deserves to live forever.

CONTENTS

III. ISRAEL

IV. AMERICA

V. GOD HAS SENT YOU

VI. THE ART OF LIVING

PREFACE

I began writing this book during the lockdown of spring 2020. Amidst the chaos, devastation, illness, and death that instantly upended life in New York City, the one silver lining of the COVID-19 pandemic was that suddenly I had time on my hands—more time to think and write than I ever had in more than thirty years as a rabbi. Aside from the occasional nervous jaunt to the supermarket or pharmacy, life in Manhattan came to a screeching halt. Everything stopped. It was eerily quiet in the city that never sleeps: serene sounds of silence punctuated only by the frequent wailing of sirens hauling yet another New Yorker to the emergency room, and all-too-often, to their graves.

At first, I did everything I could think of to engage the congregation. I directed our staff to stay connected with the thousands of members of our synagogue, many of whom left New York and were scattered throughout the country. We contacted them all day, every day. I simply went through the congregational roster alphabetically—twice—and called or emailed each member.

But as the weeks wore on, and it became increasingly clear that the pandemic would not end quickly, people settled into a routine. Their contact with us dwindled. They, too, were isolated, and their lives, like ours, slowed and narrowed, each of us trying to sustain professional and social relationships by repurposing our energy and contorting our personality into boxes on a screen. "Flattening the curve"—the constant refrain of public health officials—meant flattening our lives. Even funerals were virtually virtual, the cemeteries prohibiting or limiting mourners from gathering by the gravesite.

And so, suddenly, I had months on end to think deeply about what I had seen and learned in my thirty-four-year rabbinic career. Congregational rabbis never have enough time. We are overwhelmed with the crush of daily demands. Most of us oversee the administrative, educational, and spiritual life of the community. We are the synagogue's chief fund raiser. We supervise large staffs. We are in constant contact with our board of trustees and lay leadership. We meet people all day: congregants in need, interfaith colleagues, and activists in the Jewish and general communities. We participate in local and national coalitions, often heading social justice and charitable initiatives. We organize, participate in, and lead missions to Israel and other destinations. We teach children, young adults, parents, and empty nesters. We preach often. We attend to the urgencies and emergencies of our congregants. We conduct regular rituals, officiating at Shabbat and festival services, brises and baby namings, bar mitzvahs, graduations, conversions, weddings, and funerals, encountering families overwhelmed by emotional intensity—some of it joyous— and some of it desperately sad and tragic.

Within this maelstrom of frenetic exertion, who has time to think deeply, let alone to write books?

� ✖ ✖

Few congregants actually know what rabbis do all week. They just assume that when they encounter us, this particular activity is the only thing we do. All rabbis have experienced some variation of an interaction with a congregant who, after a sermon, asks us what else we did during the week. Sometimes there is a bite of sarcasm in their voice—as if to suggest, "You had all week to work on that sermon, and that's the best you can do?"

I say this not in criticism or complaint. To the contrary, it is the life we signed up for. Ours is a public-facing profession. Temperamentally, congregational rabbis want—and need—to be in the arena, where the action is. Most of us are not inclined toward scholarship. We want to be in the thick of things.

I realized that I would never be an academic in my last week of rabbinical school. To encourage academically-minded ordainees to consider a career of scholarship, my Bible professor invited his colleague to review for our class the doctoral dissertation he had just completed on the word "*tov*" (meaning "good") in the Bible. He spoke to us for seventy minutes about his thesis. As the class wound down, he summarized his five years of research with these words: "In sum, when the Bible mentions the word '*tov*,' it means 'good,' and where it says '*tov* me'od,' it means 'very good.'"

At that moment, I knew for sure that I would never be able to devote my life to scholarship.

I didn't have it in me. At best, I would read theses summaries of colleagues who possess the single-minded intellectual patience necessary to produce painstaking scholarly research.

But the kind of knowledge that community rabbis acquire is exceptionally useful and important in today's hyper-technological world. In an era of increasing specialization, congregational clergy are among the last remaining generalists. When my wife had bunion surgery, we sought the city's best and most knowledgeable bunion specialist. It didn't matter to us whether he knew history, read poetry, or thought deeply about the meaning of life. The surgeon we selected was regarded as the foremost expert on feet from the ankle down. That is all he did in his professional life—I called him the "from-the-ankle-down doctor." He knew just about everything there was to know about human beings from the ankle down.

Unlike the specialists of our day, who know so much about so little, congregational clergy need to know at least a little about so much. Our knowledge of the human condition comes not only from books, but through observation. We are no closer to God than anyone else. Rabbis are not *kohanim*—the ancient priests—who served as intermediaries between the people and the Almighty. Our ordination diploma provides no special access to wisdom. We are, like everyone else, the product of our times, reflecting our era's strengths and weaknesses, and our individual potential and limitations.

But what we have that others do not is a unique vantage point from which to observe human nature. Our professional lives are enmeshed in thousands of other lives. Over time, this provides us with a deeper understanding of the lived experiences of human beings. We are part of almost everything that happens in life: good and evil, tragedies, hardships, pain, suffering, envy, rage, compassion, love, friendship, generosity, kindness, and joy.

This book is an effort to make sense of what I have seen and what I have learned: to understand better the fundamental values at play in every human interaction, and to apply Jewish wisdom to our individual and communal lives. Judaism has something to say about practically every human condition, action, and motivation. While rabbis often fall short of Jewish demands, and of our own expectations, we do make an effort to see the world through the prism of Jewish teachings and to hold ourselves accountable to Jewish values.

I still remember the conversation I had with a congregant my first year as a rabbi. He came into my office, looked around at all the books on the shelves (it was a tenth of my current collection), and commented: "I don't have time to read all these books, but I want you to read them and tell me what's in them."

⚹ ⚹ ⚹

With more time suddenly available to me, I reflected on the passage of time itself. Where did the last three-plus decades go? How could they have dissipated so quickly? I began to understand in a visceral and emotional way what many others have described: time is our most precious possession. We cannot master time; it masters us.

We are losing time all the time. We expect our investments, property, and financial resources to increase. We add relatives, friends, and acquaintances to our social circles. Even if we suffer business or relationship setbacks, we can start over and replenish the numbers. But we cannot increase our allotment of time. I can never recapture the time it took to write this book. I cannot bring the time back. It is gone forever. Our lives are finite, and our time is limited. A person who lives to the age of ninety will have 32,850 days on Earth. Every day depletes the reserves. As Shakespeare put in the mouth of King Richard II: "I wasted time, and now doth time waste me."[1]

Imperceptibly at first, and then with irresistible momentum, the years accelerate with increasing speed. Noiselessly, inaudibly, and thievishly the decades whiz by. How to find the words—how to absorb—that thirty-four years have come and gone since I received my now-faded ordination diploma?

In many ways, I still feel thirty. I listen to the same music. Some time ago, my wife and I attended an Eric Clapton concert. Sitting next to us were two young people probably in their early twenties. I was curious: What was the attraction of Eric Clapton for kids in their twenties? Clapton, in his seventies, was at Madison Square Garden to celebrate his fifty-year career.

Before the concert began, I asked the couple: "Do you and your friends like Clapton?"

"Clapton is okay," said the young man, "but I'm also here for the first act—Gary Clark."

I said, "Who?"

---

1   William Shakespeare, *Richard II*, 5.5.50, https://shakespeare. folger.edu/shakespeares-works/richard-ii/act-5-scene-5/.

He gave me the same look I get when I ask for computer advice from someone his age—a kind of bewildered but respectful stare—bespeaking the unbridgeable chasm of ignorance between us. He patiently explained: "Gary Clark Jr. is a great blues guitarist—but much younger than Clapton."

And then—so earnestly, so sweetly, so innocently—with his date nodding her approval—he added: "Gary Clark is about thirty—he's in the prime of his life!"

In the prime of his life! At thirty! I felt like saying: "Hey kid—so what do you think a sixty-year old rabbi is—ancient?"—until I reminded myself that this was precisely what I thought of sixty-year-old rabbis at his age.

At some point in our lives, we realize that we will lose our race against time. This is when we begin reflecting in earnest on the passage of time.

✂ ✂ ✂

What, if anything, lasts? What really matters? Eternity came before me and eternity will come after me. What, then, is the significance of my small life within this vast expanse of cosmic infinity?

Religious thinkers are not alone in seeking to understand human meaning. Poets, authors, philosophers, and playwrights have always sought to address the central questions of the human condition. The best of them had a religious disposition, even if they, themselves, were not religious. They sought to place our lives in perspective, not of the moment, but of eternity: to rise above the temporal and corporeal, to transcend the gravitational weight of our daily toil.

This quest to understand human nature did not begin with us, and it will not end with us. Most of our questions are not new. They have been addressed by the geniuses of our species for millennia. While we have advanced by leaps and bounds technologically and scientifically since antiquity, fundamentally, we are the same creatures, with the same wants, needs, desires, emotions, and impulses. It is why ancient myths and legends speak to us. We recognize ourselves in them.

Our age imposes a unique urgency upon the human quest for meaning. We live in an era of explosive change and mass confusion. We are increasingly adrift, unmoored from institutions that anchored us in the past. We do not know where to turn or whom to trust. We do not know what—or whom—to believe. We have lost faith in the political, educational, and religious authorities we once relied upon to guide us through thickets of moral dilemmas. We hunger for moral stability.

We know, deep down, that we will not find the answers we seek by worshipping the false gods of our age. We know that a 280-character screed will not ennoble us. We know that a fifteen-second clip from a celebrity influencer will not uplift us. Most of us do not seek to empty challenge from our lives but to challenge the emptiness of life: we do not wish to escape struggle but to struggle with escapism. We want our lives to count. We want to make a difference, to leave a mark. We know, deep down, that the meaning of life is a life of meaning, that devotion to life is a life of devotion, and the promise of life is a life of promise.

According to Jewish tradition, when the Israelites crossed the Red Sea, some of them only looked down at the sea floor.

All they saw was mud and muck, and it reminded them of the slave pits of Egypt. They were in the midst of the great deliverance, and all they could think of was slavery. Others, however, looked up, and because they looked up, they witnessed salvation.

This book is an attempt to look up.

Ammiel Hirsch
New York, August 2022

I.

FAITH

THE BIG BANG

In the beginning, God created the heavens and the earth.

(Genesis 1:1)

Religion can never be in conflict with science. The facts can never be blasphemous. God cannot contradict Himself. Religion can only be ennobled by scientific knowledge. Religious people should await with eager anticipation any scientific breakthrough that can help explain the mysteries of the universe and advance our understanding of our place within it. At its best, religion embraces science as a partner, whose rigorous methodologies and standards of proof allow for a deeper, more mature religious approach.

The great fallacy of modern times is that so many look to the Bible to justify science. The Bible was never intended to be a physics textbook. The Big Bang of Genesis is not the expansion of the physical universe from a tiny ball of matter, but the expansion of the moral universe toward values that matter. Genesis is not the first chapter in Physics 101. It is the first chapter in religion. The central purpose of the first chapter of Genesis is to establish the principle that humans are different from every other living being on Earth.

The questions religion asks are different from those of science. "Was the world really created in six days?" "Did the snake really talk?" These questions are almost beside the point. They relate only to the most elementary and simple-minded curiosities. We seek much deeper meaning. We do not seek to discover the scientific truth of how the physical universe came into being. We seek to discern the moral truths of the human universe. What are the fundamental characteristics of the human creature? What is our makeup, our personality, our disposition? Who are we?

Science asks, "Is it correct?" Religion asks, "Is it good?" Science asks, "Is it factually right?" Religion asks, "Is it morally right?" Science is about particles. Religion is about poetry. For religion, "to be or not to be" is the question. Science teaches through numbers. Religion teaches through music, symbols, and parables. Science uses chemical equations. Religion uses moral equations. Science tells us what is; religion tells us what ought to be. Science is about how we got here. Religion is about why we got here. Science explains. Religion illuminates. Science convinces. Religion animates.

We are both gifted and burdened with a relentless need to understand—a need that cannot be satisfied by science alone. We are interested not only in facts, but meaning; not only knowledge, but understanding. Our questions are different from those pursuing scientific inquiry: not—What is the chemical makeup of the human creature? But *What is Man that you have regard for us? What are we that you are mindful of us?* We ask not "how we were born," but *Why did I come out of this womb?*

Science and religion are not contradictory but complementary, companions in the human quest for understanding. A religious person who denies the facts converts his faith into fantasy. A scientist who denies the possibility of God limits the horizons of possibilities. Albert Einstein wrote, "Science without religion is lame, religion without science is blind." Science does not carry you to the end, it merely gives a glimpse of the endlessness of the horizon.

The whole point of science is to unlock the mechanism of the world. Einstein felt that there was a fundamental cause of all existence, and although he never found it, he never ceased searching. He felt that nature was not accidental—"God does not play dice with the universe"—but that there were set laws that governed the natural world.

Why would it be damaging to faith if we discovered these laws? Why do the discoveries of the laws of gravity or the Big Bang contradict the belief in God? To the contrary, such discoveries enhance faith because they allow us to peer into the Mind of God; to comprehend how it was all put together.

I have never fully understood why anyone but a fundamentalist literalist would be troubled by evolution. Who decided that the most fundamentalist approach to religion is the most fundamentally sound one? The SARS-CoV-2 virus that led to the COVID-19 pandemic, like every other virus, constantly evolved and mutated. Every mutation further validated Darwin's theory. Even human beings can create evolution. We breed dogs, horses, and other animals. Over time, selective breeding altered their makeup. So if we can do it, why can't God?

Darwin asked how species evolved. He never intended to propose a moral theory of why they evolved. Darwin did not destroy God; he only destroyed a deeply flawed conception of God. No modern-thinking person, especially those seeking to make religious sense of the world, can suspend reason whenever a dinosaur bone is found.

Genesis teaches that there is a God. God is a creator. There is an order to the universe. Human beings are the pinnacle of creation, made in the image of God, but we are not God. Genesis teaches that human beings have free will and that part of this freedom includes the capacity to choose evil. We learn from Genesis that life is good and that there is meaning and purpose to human existence. *Do what is right and good in the sight of God*—this is what Genesis teaches. The concept of good is not a scientific term; it is a religious and moral term. We possess not only an organ called a heart: we have heart. Our bodies contain not only cells, but a soul. We have consciousness in a biological sense, but not only that. Religion teaches that we have a conscience. *My conscience admonishes me at night*, the Psalmist wrote.

We are creatures meant for God. *Seek Me and live*, the prophet Amos urged. Faith is native to us. It is rooted in that place in our composition that makes us human. We are not more advanced or sophisticated by embracing only one side of the human personality—the side of reason and judgment—while suppressing the other side of our personality—the side of emotion, intuition, and feeling. Both are part of our human nature. Both are critical to the acquisition of knowledge and understanding.

Reason, cold hard reason, is only part of our makeup. It is only one way we learn, but not the only way; it is only one way we know, but not the only way. Imagination, love, hate, feeling, passion, and intuition—these are also forms of knowledge. French philosopher Alexis de Tocqueville wrote, "There is no philosopher in the world…that does not believe in a million things on faith." "Faith is synonymous with working hypothesis," wrote William James. Faith begins where proof ends. We take a leap of faith when we have no other satisfying explanation. Faith is knowledge too, but it is not scientific knowledge. It is possible to know God, but it is not possible to prove God by current scientific standards of proof.

Science cannot even begin to provide answers to all of the questions of science, let alone questions outside its interests or expertise. There is so much more that we do not know about existence than that which we do know. Science has taught us how expansive the universe is and how little we know of it. Moreover, there are questions that science will never even raise, let alone answer. The poet read his poem to the mathematician, who, upon reflection, responded to the poet, "What does that prove?"

Religion is not an exercise in mathematical proof. You cannot get absolute answers by consulting a religion textbook. Even religious people make this mistake. They simplify the religious task and reduce it to the most basic and literal perspective. We should fight the temptation to Google-ize religion. We cannot go to a religious website and instantly find the answer. Our purpose is not information alone, but inspiration.

Religion is the repository of the most penetrating questions, the most passionate emotions, and the most intense dreads and dreams of Mankind. It is the place where we embark upon the quest for meaning. It is the path, the journey, and the search that most characterize religion, not the arrival. The Talmud explains that one receives an additional reward for going to a more distant synagogue, because part of the drawing toward God is in the journey.

If we understand that the religious task is to ponder the deepest mysteries of the universe, to ask the hardest questions, then we must also appreciate that we will not be able to find all of the answers. Faith is about believing even when we cannot answer the question. It is faith in the voyage. This was the faith of Abraham. He did not even know where he was going. *Go forth to a land that I will show you*, is all he knew. This is the faith of the strong—the courage to believe without answers: *Take your son Isaac and ascend one of the mountains that I will show you*. The religious journey has meaning, even if we do not find the certainty we seek. It is not a journey to nowhere. We are not fighting windmills quixotically, or endlessly waiting for Godot. There is arrival, too, even if we cannot fully conceive of the destination.

There is a passage in the Talmud that states that a baby learns all it needs to know while in its mother's womb. Upon the birth of the child, a heavenly presence descends from on high and taps the baby above the lip (which explains the groove above our upper lip), causing it to forget everything it learned during gestation. The Sages thus suggest that life's task is to recover the essential truths we already knew at the dawn of creation. We yearn to go home, to restore ourselves to that source of energy and harmony that gave us life.

Like any great odyssey, the religious quest is a journey home.

THE BIG BANG OF DESTRUCTION

*Behold, the Lord God has His eye upon the sinful
kingdom: I will wipe it off the face of the earth.*

(Amos 9:8)

The sad truth of the human condition is that while we have advanced spectacularly in the realm of science, we have advanced slowly in the realm of morals. The profound failings that drove the Hebrew prophets to moral fulminations plague us today as well.

Our lack of moral progress means that we are constantly at risk of destruction. The very technology that liberated could destroy. We are the first human beings capable of exterminating our own race through scientifically engineered weapons of mass destruction or ecological catastrophe. Science gives with one hand and takes with the other. Our increasing reliance on technology has made us increasingly vulnerable to it. Morality, not technology, is still the key to a peaceful world. It is still the bulwark of our liberty.

As President Franklin D. Roosevelt famously said: "Today we are faced with the pre-eminent fact that, if civilization is to survive, we must cultivate the science of human relationships—the ability of all peoples, of all kinds, to live together and work together in the same world, at peace."[2] The more we advance technologically, the harder it is to remember our purpose. With every technological advance, we lose something. I used to be an expert in navigation. In the military, I could find a sand dune in the middle of the desert by reading the stars in the dark of night. There was something almost mystical about that. Today, we plug in the coordinates and our GPS takes us there. Navigation is a lost art. Who even brings maps anymore on a road trip? It is so much easier today. We drive straight to our hotel, rather than the old days when we had to circle the unknown streets of a foreign city for hours, testing the patience and drawing the ire of local drivers.

But we now conflate the speed of arrival with the purpose of the journey. What is our quest? This is the human question. No technology can answer this. We choose the destination. GPS only takes us to the place that we selected. It does not tell us why this destination and not another. The only navigation software that works to address human purpose is our moral positioning system that, by its nature, is un-mechanized, un-mechanical, and unassailable. Kindness cannot be measured by click-throughs. Google has not made us grateful. Facebook has not made us forgiving. Reddit has not made us righteous. Social media has not made us committed to social justice.

2   Franklin D. Roosevelt, "Undelivered Address Prepared for Jefferson Day," The American Presidency Project, originally written April 13, 1945, https://www.presidency.ucsb.edu/documents/undelivered-address-prepared-for-jefferson-day.

Science is morally neutral. We are no more honest than when Moses brought down the tablets millennia ago. In fact, we may even be less honest, because the temptations are greater. Technology has made it so much easier to cheat. A hacker can break into our bank account without leaving home. The damage inflicted from such a corrupted soul could be many times worse than in the pre-technological age. What is the use of Kindle access to all the philosophies ever written if it does not kindle in us moral awareness?

Here is the irony: what was intended to advance human freedom often has the opposite result. Today, we can read practically every word ever written—the entire library of humanity in our pocket. It was supposed to make us smart. So why are so many so dumb? With all the scientific data at our disposal, how do we explain such widespread science denial? We are still prone to magical thinking, even if we now express it technologically to the thousands we euphemistically, and a bit sadly, call "friends."

We have been liberated to express ourselves with almost no limitation. But so have they. And they have not been freed of superstition or hate. Technology empowers intolerance. Terrorists use Twitter. The very science that propels us to gleaming new ages has also returned us to dark Middle Ages. Anti-Semites and haters of every kind use social media. How ridiculous it now seems to have hoped that the Holocaust would once and for all purge the human heart of hatred of Jews. The human creature does not change so quickly. We are what we always were: admirable, good, kind, noble in reason, the beauty of the world, the pinnacle of all creation.

And, at the same time, we are "Most ignorant of what [we are] most assured,/ [Our] glassy essence, like an angry ape/ Plays such fantastic tricks before high heaven/ As makes the angels weep."[3] Liberty, the value that underpins advanced civilizations and facilitates scientific breakthroughs;—that allows for art, music, culture, medicine, and society;—also empowers those who undermine liberty, who seek a Hobbesian world where there are "no arts, no letters, no society; and worst of all, continual fear of violent death; and the life of Man solitary, poor, nasty, brutish and short."[4] The very technology that promised to bring us closer, to unite us in common purpose, to create global virtual communities, also polarizes us. The explosion of websites offering every view under the sun has allowed us to pick and choose whom we want to hear. We can tune out everyone else. Often, it is not truth we pursue, but comfort: the false comfort of the echo chamber.

Of course, I am not against technology. I like air conditioning and indoor plumbing. Jewish tradition is emphatic that if you are not feeling well, you should not put your fate in miracles. Go to a doctor, fool. Get vaccinated. Just to contemplate what science, technology, and medicine will gift to the human race by the end of the 21st century causes my heart to skip, and I lament that I will not be around to see it.

---

3   William Shakespeare, *Measure for Measure*, 2.2.148-151, https://shakespeare.folger.edu/shakespeares-works/measure-for-measure/?_ga=2.125900941.1671216703.1663867231-1221077582.1663867231.

4   Thomas Hobbs, *Leviathan*, (Seattle: Pacific Publishing Studio, 2011), https://www.google.com/books/edition/Leviathan/RfAxXwAACAAJ?hl=en.

At the same time, we must recognize the extraordinary risks we take in putting all of our eggs in the basket of science. The most critical danger facing the world today, in both military and ecological terms, is that our technological capacities have outstripped our moral capacities. Continuing rapid technological progress without corresponding moral progress will bring destruction beyond anything our world has experienced. We need moral training to enhance and augment our technological training. We seek not only a bright and active mind but also a *discerning and knowing heart*—a *listening heart to distinguish between good and bad.*

Are we exploiting technology, or is technology exploiting us? Are we using technology to enhance our creativity, or is technology so overwhelming our innate personalities that we have become automatons—dumb, dull, boorish, and boring? Is technology enslaving or liberating us?

With every advance, we give something away. Our vast progress has caused a palpable loss of reverence. Some of the mystery of the world has evaporated before our eyes. We cannot look at a summer thunderstorm in quite the same way as the ancients did: *The God of glory thunders, the Lord over the mighty waters…the voice of God shatters the cedars of Lebanon.… The Lord sat enthroned at the Flood.*

Or, as Mark Twain put it:

"We have not the reverent feeling for the rainbow… because we know how it is made. We have lost as much as we gained by prying into that matter."

CAUGHT IN THE MAZE

Stand by the road, ask the good way and
walk on it, and find rest for your souls.

(Jeremiah 6:16)

Franz Kafka wrote a compelling short story:

"Alas," said the mouse, "the world is growing smaller every day. At the beginning it was so big that I was afraid, I kept running and running, and I was glad when at last I saw walls far away to the right and left, but these long walls have narrowed so quickly that I am in the last chamber already, and there in the corner stands the trap that I must run into."

"You only need to change your direction," said the cat, and ate it up[5].

Kafka called this tale, "A Little Fable." I interpret it as a little fable on life. At the beginning, the world is so big that we find ourselves lost inside the bigness of it all. But as the years

---

5   Franz Kafka, "A Little Fable," 1920, https://www.babelmatrix.org/ works/de/Kafka%2C_Franz-1883/Kleine_Fabel/en/34801-A_Little_Fable

unfold, and we keep running and running, the walls seem to close in on us. We run toward a goal, or run away from danger, disappointment, disease, and death. We cannot stop running. The walls of life keep closing in.

We run the same track every day, rising at dawn, running to answer emails; running to work; running at work; running to the gym; running at the gym; running to take care of the kids; running to pick them up from school, camp, soccer; running home to prepare dinner. And then, in bed, and all over again. Month after month, year after year. At some point, we seek to explain, and ultimately, escape, our predicament. We want to find the way out—to give meaning and purpose to our infinitesimal smallness within the colossal bigness of the universe.

✼ ✼ ✼

Most Americans choose one of two avenues of escape.

The first is the path of science and technology. These have empowered us as never before. We believe we have the capacity to resolve any ailment—physical, emotional, psychological, or sociological. We assume that there is a scientific explanation to everything, and hence, a scientific solution to every problem. The meaning of life is not a philosophical or religious problem, it is a scientific one, and we now have science-based solutions. The way out of the maze is to plow ahead: to roll over all the hidden obstacles and lurking predators by discovering the scientific essence of things. We can invent our way out of the existential anxiety most of us will feel at some point in our lives.

Many believe that we are well on our way to overpowering and ultimately conquering nature. We can already predict storms, earthquakes, and droughts, and this capacity will improve in decades to come. We know how to build earthquake-resistant structures. We learned how to desalinate water from the sea and make the desert bloom. We bend rivers to our will. We harness the sun, the wind, and molecules to produce immense energy. Those of us who live in cities hardly know nature's wrath. Drought was the terror of the ancient world, causing famine and death. The Israelites ended up enslaved in Egypt because of drought. It changed the course of Jewish history. Today, in America, our bigger problem is over-consumption. More Americans will die from obesity than starvation.

Until the modern era, almost everyone came into this world and departed this world never experiencing anything but their own village or town. Today, we have conquered the skies so thoroughly that we hardly think twice of the miracle of hurtling through clouds in a metal tube to the furthest reaches of the globe. For eons, we were prisoners of gravity, wondering what was out there. Our ancestors looked to the heavens, dreaming of "[slipping] the surly bonds of Earth [to]...the high untrespassed sanctity of space...[to touch] the face of God."[6] Reaching the stars was so fanciful that the mere speculation was evidence of human hubris. Icarus received his just reward by crashing to the earth. Today, we take space travel for granted. In the coming centuries, humans will explore the distant reaches of the universe.

---

6   John Gillespie Magee, *High Flight*, https://www.poetryfoundation. org/poems/157986/high-flight-627d3cfb1e9b7.

The science of modern communications is a thing of miraculous beauty. It is stunning to think that we can communicate instantly with almost everyone in the world. From the days that the Sumerians first invented writing, human beings endeavored to bridge the chasm of ignorance and distance separating one individual, one society, from another. Until the invention of the telegraph, less than two centuries ago, human messengers or carrier pigeons delivered news. Pheidippides had to run from Marathon to Athens to deliver news of the victory over the Persians. Today, in one hour, we can organize mass protests half a world away.

Medicine has revolutionized our lives. Lifespans have increased dramatically. We are healthier than ever. A hundred years ago, we could die of a sore throat. Some scientists now foresee the conquest of natural death. While in centuries to come, people may still die from accidents, wars, crimes, and natural disasters, scientists predict that eventually we will discover why cells age and die, and intervene genetically to stave off illness and mortality. At that point, we will have the power of the gods: immortality. Science will succeed where religion and philosophy failed to resolve the central problem of mortality. We will eliminate the problem altogether, thus obviating the need to explain it. There will be no need to feel the anxiety of mortality.

So it is not surprising that so many people look to science to provide all the answers to our most pressing questions. Even existential angst is a medical problem, not a philosophical one. If not now, then at some point in the future, we will invent a pill that will rewire our brains so that we never feel anxiety. Technology will replace religion, philosophy, psychology, and sociology. It is already happening. Computers can produce music that is indistinguishable to most people from the best of Beethoven. No person on Earth can defeat the most advanced computer chess champion.

But if science so empowers us, why do we feel so weak, lonely, broken, and adrift? If we now can know everything, why do we feel so ignorant, fragile, and alienated from others and from ourselves? If we know so much about the human brain, why do our minds trouble us so? If we are filled with so much knowledge, why do we feel so empty?

� ✺ ✺

In his book, *Homo Deus*, Yuval Noah Harari asserts that modernity is a deal that all of us sign onto. "The entire contract," he wrote, "can be summarized in a single phrase: Humans agree to give up meaning in exchange for power."[7]

In other words, science has so empowered us that we now know for sure that there is no higher meaning to existence. We have given up dreaming of Paradise for the power to create paradise on Earth. We relinquish the belief in life after death for the power to create life without death. We already slipped the "surely bonds of Earth" half a century ago, and we know that there is nothing out there—certainly not the face of God. Science teaches that there is no cosmic plan. There is no purpose. We now know how we got here. Creation is unguided and unintended. We evolved chaotically, haphazardly, and coincidentally. There is no rhyme or reason to suf-

---

7   Yuval Noah Harari, *Homo Deus* (New York: Harper Collins, 2017).

fering. There is no rhyme or reason to anything. Everything just is. Humans are insignificant talking apes on an insignificant rock, a tiny speck in the vastness of space. We are the product of random chaos.

How liberating! Science discovered the way out of the maze of life.

We suffer, not because of some higher purpose or Higher Being. We suffer because we haven't yet found the cure to this particular physical, emotional, or sociological ailment. The only thing holding us back is our own ignorance. There is no God to punish us. There is no master plan to frustrate us. We acquire ever-more power in a universe that has ever-less meaning.

But how empowered are we, really? How many hours a day do most Americans spend watching a screen? Are we even able to resist its hypnotic hold over us? Is that empowerment or servitude? Nowadays, people walk the streets, their heads buried in a phone called "smart" that makes them so dumb that equally distracted drivers often run them over. If space aliens were to visit us from a distant planet, not knowing anything about the human race, would they conclude that we are the masters of the screen—or that the screen masters us? They might surmise that this device must have some mesmerizing grip over human beings. We can't pull away. Our data intrigues us even more than our dinner date. Is that freedom or servitude?

And they accuse religion of being the opium of the masses! It seems to me that many more people are addicted to Google than God.

Modern communications, social media, and the internet have indeed empowered humanity immensely. We now have all of human knowledge in the palm of our hand. It should have made us wise, informed, knowledgeable. But is that really the case? Are we more open, more tolerant, more educated—or do we spend most of our time in the echo chamber with people who agree with us? Does social media make us a bigger, better, and more content human family, or are we more polarized than ever?

Even if we have all the knowledge of the world at our disposal, do we know what to do with it? Does it liberate or paralyze? Does it clarify or confuse? Knowledge is power, but it is a power that can be turned against us as well. I have so much information available to me that I do not know how to process it. I have so many options on Netflix that I can't choose. I often flick around the net after work and fall asleep not having watched anything.

There was something very 21st century about the 2016 Russian interference in our elections. Their method was not censorship. They did not try to block information. To the contrary, they flooded America with so much information that we could not distinguish between what was real and what was fake. We could not separate the wheat from the chaff—the truly important from the trivial or fictitious.

Airplanes, indeed, empowered us enormously. We can reach the furthest points on the earth in less than a day. But they can reach us as well. They can fly these airplanes into buildings and drop death from the sky. Is that empowering or weakening? After 9/11, we cannot look at a passenger plane in quite the same innocent, peaceful, and empowering way as before.

Fossil fuels fueled a great leap in human technological power. But we have also polluted the skies, the drinking water, the very air we breathe. We are on the verge of ecological catastrophe. Have we conquered the problem of human existence or complicated it? Nuclear physics created enormous energy, enabling our deepest desires for power. It also created the bomb. Our empowerment has empowered us to destroy everything.

Medicine has so advanced that it has released us from the chains of pain. But more of us than ever are addicted to pain medication. Computers, indeed, have liberated us. But it is a double-edged sword. It is not only that we cannot disconnect; more disconcerting, the machines determine how we live. Steve Jobs told me that I need a smart phone to live a productive life. I didn't reason myself into Apple devices. Am I stronger or weaker as a result? Am I more empowered or more adrift?

C.S. Lewis wrote:

Each new power won by man is a power over man. Each advance leaves him weaker as well as stronger. We give up our soul to get power in return. But once our souls, that is, ourselves, have been given up, the power thus conferred will not belong to us. We shall in fact be the slaves and puppets of that to which we have given our souls…. If a man chooses to treat himself as raw material, raw material he will be.

If I have sold my soul to the machine, the power I receive in return does not belong to me. Google, Facebook, and Amazon are the masters of what I do with my life. I am merely the raw material. Even if I am bored and just surfing YouTube, the algorithms determine what I will watch, how I will spend my time. The algorithms influence what I want and what I buy. Nowadays, algorithms even choose our life partners.

I am not anti-science. To the contrary, I would much rather live in these times than any other time in history. I like to travel on planes—or at least to arrive quickly at distant lands. I prefer avocados at the supermarket than having to grow my own. I cannot imagine life without computers. But we have been so seduced by the empowerment of science that we run the risk of turning the very science that so confidently asserts there is no God into a god.

Until the modern era, the human problem was how to align ourselves to the reality of the world. We did that through discipline, morals, justice, a sense of right and wrong, and an intuition of the eternal. Now, so many expect to align the world to themselves. Take the pill and you won't feel sad. We can eliminate sadness. Rewire your prefrontal cortex and you will avoid the crime. We can eliminate crime, violence, and injustice through science. When the technology improves, we can hand over all our decisions to Artificial Intelligence, which will know us better than we know ourselves, and will never get tired, emotional, or feel conflicted.

It is a kind of nihilism. We give up real meaning in exchange for the illusion of power. How to save a life from killer viruses—that is a question for science. Why save that life? What is the worth of that life? What value do we ascribe to that life? These are religious, poetic, and philosophical questions.

We have become mechanical, soulless. Modern economics has generated so much affluence—at least for some of us—that we now have to figure out what to do with all our free time. Boredom has become another affliction to overcome in our hyperactive era. We need to be on all the time—we can't waste time—as if frenetic activity in pursuit of a hollow goal is not wasting time. As if spending a fortnight playing Fortnite is not wasting time.

We forget that the most meaningful moments of our lives often seem trivial, even boring when we lived them: that uninterrupted afternoon on the beach with our family; lounging around the house, just talking or reading or listening to music. When, as a teenager, I endured another boring Shabbat afternoon in Jerusalem not doing anything but sitting around listening to people talk, sometimes in languages that I did not even understand, it seemed deadly. But now, looking back, I don't remember the boredom. I remember all the people I loved who are no more. I remember my mother singing her beloved Russian songs. The memory of my mother singing—an inconsequential event at that time—is so meaningful to me today. I wish I could hear my mother sing again: just once—just one of those songs she loved so much.

By presuming that physics, biology, and chemistry can explain all reality, we are losing the sense of transcendence—

the essential component of what it means to be human. Is there really nothing more to loyalty than self-interest? Is there nothing more to empathy than selfishness? Is altruism merely brain connections, and we can manipulate any brain to be altruistic? No wonder so many are so alienated and in such despair. There is nothing sacred. Nothing profound. Is there nothing more to love than the firing of brain synapses, adrenalin, dopamine, hormones, and chemicals? What about the poetry of love?

How do I love thee? Let me count the ways.
I love thee to the depth and breadth and height
My soul can reach....
I love thee freely...I love thee purely...I love thee with
the passion....
I love thee with the breath,
Smiles, tears, of all my life.[8]

The more we advance technologically, the greater is the urgency to avoid desacralizing human existence. We must work even harder to preserve, protect, defend, and deepen the sense of human grandeur, the spark of the divine within us. We are much too confident in our knowledge. We know a lot. We know incomparably more than we used to. But that is all we know. We don't know anything else—which is most of what there is to know.

---

8   Elizabeth Barrett Browning, "How Do I Love Thee? Sonnet 43," 1850, https://poets.org/poem/how-do-i-love-thee-sonnet-43.

Some people, recognizing the inability of science and technology to answer the central questions of existence, choose another way of escaping the maze of life: resignation. It is the opposite of power. Those pursuing this route believe that the only way to avoid despair is to withdraw. Stop running. Stop fighting. Do not take anything too seriously. Resign yourself to the inevitable—a hard, painful existence that ends in death.

There are both religious and secular versions of this philosophy.

Some religions emphasize the world to come over this world. This world is hopeless and irredeemable. We run toward some unachievable destination because we mistake the true destination. Our purpose is not this pitiful world filled with suffering and discontent. Running will only lead to more walls, more traps, more despair. Our true destination is heaven. These philosophies assert that power is an illusion. No invention, no discovery, no breakthrough will save us. Give yourself up to our ultimate destination: Paradise.

In this post-religious era, many of us pursue the secular version of the philosophy of resignation. Its central teaching is happiness. Don't worry, be happy. We are all going to die anyway. So focus on yourself. At least while I live, I will live happy. Let those other sorry souls suffer.

In *Les Miserables*, Victor Hugo puts these words in the mouth of a senator speaking to the Bishop of Digne:

> The immortality of man is a daydream. What nonsense it all is. God is a grotesque humbug. What am I but

an organized handful of dust? I have a choice. I can
suffer or enjoy. Where will suffering end? In oblivion,
and I shall have suffered. Where will enjoyment end?
Also in oblivion but [at least] I shall have enjoyed...
The only thing to do is to...use yourself while you
have yourself.

So many of us live that way. We use ourselves to the limit
while we still have our strength. In pursuit of happiness, we
chase money, success, fame, pleasure, consumption, ease, luxury. We convince ourselves that if only we had this one thing,
we would be happy.

Samuel Johnson imagined a place called Happy Valley.
Everything that could make people sad was excluded from
the valley. The inhabitants of Happy Valley devoted their
lives solely to pleasure. The young prince, Rasselas, became
dissatisfied with having all his desires granted. As soon as he
wanted something, he had it—and this created in him a state
of despair. He decided to escape Happy Valley, and after many
months and much searching, he found the secret way out.
Rasselas traveled the world for many years. He discovered that
no one achieves happiness. Ultimately, he returned to Happy
Valley—unhappy—but at least less unhappy than the other
miserable souls he met in his travels.

Beware the high priests of happiness. Herman Melville
told the parable of the death of an Ohio honey-hunter who,
seeking honey in the crotch of a hollow tree, found such
exceeding store of it—that leaning too far over, it sucked him
in so that he died—embalmed in honey. The lure of honey
entraps. The more we find, the more we want. We are never

satisfied. Human beings have an infinite longing. Once a desire is satisfied, we want more. This longing, this drive for more, can entomb us. As too much honey leads to physical ailments, too much pleasure leads to a diabetic spirit. It is why the American founders brilliantly defined one of our entitlements as not happiness itself, but the *pursuit* of happiness. They realized that if we ever actually found happiness—like Rasselas—we would be miserable.

While the self-help shelves overflow with advice on doing this one thing that will make you happy, in truth, the happiness specialists of our days are, themselves, the product of the confusions of our times. We are too complicated, compromised, conceited, competitive, and combative to be satisfied with the happiness elixir pedaled by popular culture.

✻ ✻ ✻

Judaism offers a third way. Of course, we believe in eternality; that there is more to our lives than what we see. The body dies; the spirit lives on with God. But we do not spend most of our time speculating about the world to come. We focus on this world. There are *mitzvot* to do—daily commandments that require engagement with others and with the many details of our own daily subsistence.

We do not reject science. We embrace science. Literalists who place themselves against progress appall us. Many of the greatest Jewish minds devoted themselves to the natural and social sciences, to research, medicine, and now technology. Science helps explain creation. The Bible cannot contradict what science conclusively proves. If science established that the world was formed over billions of years, the biblical passage of the six days of creation cannot be literally true.

We do not reject secular power. To the contrary, much of Jewish thought is devoted to how to exercise power morally. Power is necessary to repair a world that often misuses power to oppress the powerless.

Nor do we reject pleasure. We embrace any technological breakthrough that has the potential to make life easier or more meaningful. Fertility clinics are filled with the most Orthodox of Jews. We believe in the future. We believe in life. Life should be enjoyed. We do not worship weakness. We do not glorify poverty. We do not venerate hardship. We are an optimistic people. We *kvetch* a lot—but if you look more deeply, our complaints reflect our commitment to the future, our belief that we can do better. Human beings do not need to be so miserable.

Judaism advanced a concept of "messiah." It originated with us. But Jews do not await the arrival of a redeemer. We force the messiah to arrive through our daily acts of repair. Salvation comes not through a savior. The savior comes through salvation. The messiah will arrive only after we have prepared the world for his arrival. As Kafka wrote, with such profound Jewish sensibilities: "The messiah will come only when he is no longer necessary. He will come the day after his arrival."

While embracing progress, while marveling at, and making use of, the brilliant achievements of science, we return time and again to those age-old principles and values that were carved out of the stone of antiquity and anchor all human life. Nothing better has been invented since, and nothing ever will be.

Love your neighbor as yourself;

What is hateful to you do not do unto others;

Honor your father and mother;

Do not murder;

Do not steal;

Do not bear false witness; do not take bribes;

Speak the truth within your heart;

Be faithful; be loyal;

Protect the stranger and the weak;

Relieve poverty: When you cut your harvest, and have forgotten a sheaf, do not go back to pick it up. It shall be for the foreigner, the fatherless and the widow.

Free the captive, redeem the oppressed; let the slave go free;

Be compassionate—may the law of kindness be on your tongue;

Pursue justice, love mercy, walk humbly.

What is the Jewish way out of Kafka's maze? How to avoid the ever-narrowing walls and the trap guarded by the cat? Not by overpowering the world, and not by escaping the world, but by persistence. Defiance. Tenacity. By finding meaning, purpose, and joy in the world as it is and ceaselessly working to create a better world. The meaning of life is a life of meaning. The purpose of life is a life of purpose. The energy of life is a life of energy. Commitment to life is a life of commitment. Devotion to life is a life of devotion. The promise of life is a life of promise.

We do not seek salvation through the worship of false gods. We do not seek escape. We do not seek, nor do we expect, a challenge-free world. We do not seek to empty challenge from our lives but to challenge the emptiness of life. Not to escape struggle but to struggle with escapism. We want our fight to count. To mean something.

We pray for strength, for the capacity to endure. Human grandeur is revealed in all its glory through the struggle to carry on.

David Foster Wallace gave this brilliant interpretation of Kafka's "Little Fable":

> The horrific struggle to establish a human self results in a self whose humanity is inseparable from that horrific struggle. That our endless and impossible journey toward home is in fact our home. We pound and pound on the door seeking admission desperate to enter—we pound and pound until it finally opens— and it opens outward—we've been inside what we've wanted all along.

LADDER TO HEAVEN

Can I take the place of God?

(Genesis 30:2)

It was a glorious sunny day when the Towers collapsed. You could see forever. The air was clear. The cooling breezes of summer's waning days had finally blown away the stifling humidity of August. This was New York at its finest. Manhattan had its groove back, and it was at maximum velocity again. The kids were in school. The adults were at work. Autumn was beckoning, and spring was in our step. On these rare days, New Yorkers and New York become one; we feel the energy of the city surging through us. Life doesn't get much better than this. To live in the greatest city in the world on one of its perfect days is to live the American dream.

At mid-morning, it grew dark in the sunshine and difficult to see. A hideous black cloud spread over the city, hovering above us for days on end. It was hard to breathe. To breathe was to inhale our loved ones, our family, our friends, and our neighbors who were incinerated by the fires.

It was a day of contrasts: light and darkness; good and evil; humanity and barbarism; civilization and anarchy; heroism and cowardice; a blue sky and The Cloud. We are creatures of contrasts. We saw the best and the worst of people on that day. We made discoveries about ourselves. From the rubble emerged a new understanding of who we are. We saw so many acts of uncommon courage, to conclude that courage is more common than we thought. We witnessed so many acts of compassion and generosity, to conclude that perhaps people really are good at heart.

For New Yorkers, most symbolic of all, testifying to everything good about humanity, were our firefighters. On that day, when heaven was falling and the earth's foundations fled, they rushed up the stairs and on their shoulders held the sky suspended. They bore the desperate hopes and final confessions of so many human beings. The pillars of the earth held a while longer in deference to their valor. Many people are alive today because of the firefighters of New York City. Even gravity pays homage to human courage. One person recounted that as he walked down with a ninety-year-old man he was assisting, he passed thirty to fifty firefighters heading up the stairs. "I don't think any of them made it," he said. "It was like a ladder to heaven."

Religion urges us to climb the ladder to heaven. We seek to rise above the forces of brutality weighing us down; to imagine a better world, a world where heaven and earth kiss and where God and humans embrace:

And Jacob dreamt, and behold there was a ladder set on the ground and its top reached the sky and the angels of God were ascending and descending. God is in this place, and that is the ladder to heaven.

Step by step, we ascend, steadily improving and repairing our world until we break through the clouds of hate that hover over our lives and darken our horizons.

What demonic force propels people to murder? What goes through the minds of those who speak of paradise in heaven and inflict hell on earth? "The mind is its own place, and in it self/ Can make a Heav'n of Hell, a Hell of Heav'n."[9] What impels the faithful, the very people who claim to serve God, to take the place of God in dispensing life and death?

C.S. Lewis wrote: "Of all bad men, religious bad men are the worst." They are the worst because when they commit transgressions, they validate immorality in the eyes of others. Instead of cleansing our impurities, they whitewash them. An act of violence becomes a righteous crusade. A murder becomes a noble jihad. The world is turned upside down through an unholy inversion of values: cruel is kind, killing is compassion, and sin is salvation. The horrible becomes honorable. Our highest aspirations are manipulated to excuse our basest impulses. "The Almighty wanted the baby killed. God decreed the collapse of the buildings."

It is not difficult to claim divine sanction for murder. Even those who have a casual understanding of religion can cite chapter and verse to justify acts of violence. There are proof texts to support any position you choose to take. Both religious abolitionists and religious slaveholders cited biblical sources. If your nature is inclined toward power, conquest, control, domination, revenge, and retribution, there are plenty

---

9   John Milton, *Paradise Lost*, 1.221-270, https://poets.org/poem/paradise-lost-book-i-lines-221-270.

of sources you can find to validate these impulses. If, on the other hand, the arc of your life bends toward goodness, compassion, understanding, kindness, and tolerance, these texts, too, exist in abundance.

In the end, it is not about citing chapter and verse; it is about establishing a mindset. At its best, religion is a source of inspiration, not intimidation. Religion is sublime when it animates us, awakening the better angels of our nature. We seek to instill a sense of right, goodness, and decency that is so overwhelming that any inconsistent thought or deed is rendered reprehensible in our eyes.

Surely, if religion is for anything, it is for life. The key insight of religion is the insistence upon the distinctiveness of the human creature. All were created by God. We alone were created in the image of God. Every religious principle flows from this axiom. If both you and I were created in God's image, we have equal sanctity, equal worth, and equal dignity.

In theory, the concept of the sanctity of human life establishes a stronger claim than even the principle of the protection of human rights enshrined in Western jurisprudence. Rights can be suspended. Lincoln suspended *habeas corpus* during the Civil War. Rights are weighed against other rights. On the other hand, sanctity exists at all times. The sanctity of life, the core religious principle, contains within it the concept of human dignity that is the center of Western jurisprudence.

Reverence for life is religion's primary preoccupation and central principle. Every life is precious. Every life is sacred. The Talmud states that to save a person's life is akin to saving the world entire, and to destroy a life is akin to destroying the world. "Whoever sheds blood destroys the image of God," proclaimed the sage Akiva.

Our age has produced wolves in sheep's clothing. Savage and cunning, they cry "peace!" but let slip the dogs of war. They claim virtue, but vice is their ally. They postulate goodness but are zealous for all that is vile. A Kafkaesque metamorphosis has occurred in our times: we awoke one morning from uneasy dreams to find religion transformed into a gigantic distortion. From their dank caves and dark hideouts, and from their gleaming sanctuaries and glistening shrines, religious extremists fling around the name of God as if the Divine were some appendage to their egotistical and perverted view of the world. Using the latest technology, the fruits of the labor of centuries of striving toward the light, they would take us back to the Dark Ages and wreak havoc and destruction on the most advanced civilizations in the history of the world. *Woe unto them who present darkness as light and light as darkness.* What took centuries to build could be destroyed in one moment of murderous madness. Millennia of human progress wiped away in the blink of an eye.

They consider themselves demigods, freely invoking the name of the Holy One to justify horrendous crimes. They bestride the narrow world like modern day Goliaths, their swords dripping with blood. There is something primal and bestial about them. You see pictures of chopped-off heads, of burnings, bombings, and knifings, and you ask yourself: from what dark place did this emerge, what is the source of such fathomless depravity? Dostoevsky wrote: "People sometimes talk about man's bestial cruelty, but that is being terribly unjust and offensive to the beasts. A beast can never be as cruel as a human being, so artistically, so picturesquely cruel. The tiger simply gnaws and tears and that is the only thing it knows. It would never enter its head to nail people to fences by their ears and leave them like that all night, even were it able to do such a thing."

How did religion become the enemy of progress? How have we become agents of intolerance, casually dishing out death and destruction? The name of God has been despoiled, dragged through the refuse of the world's most fanatical deviants. For many today, God represents bigotry, oppression of women, violence, and rage. How trippingly do the basest impulses of human beings form on the lips of those who swear loyalty to a higher cause! So-called holy men invoke heaven to perpetrate the most earthly crimes. *Would you murder and also inherit?*

They are about rebellion, not religion. They are about superstition, not sanctity. By invoking divine authority, they arrogate to themselves powers not theirs. *Am I God to give life and deal death?* They speak for themselves, not God. They act for themselves, not God. They represent themselves, not God. It is their needs they pursue, not God's needs. It is their flaws they exhibit, not God's flaws. It is ambition disguising itself as a calling. Religion is the veneer. As Milton put it: "To reign is worth ambition though in Hell:/ Better to reign in Hell, than serve in Heav'n."[10]

Edmund Burke, reflecting on the French Revolution, wrote:

---

10 John Milton, *Paradise Lost*, 1.221-270, https://poets.org/poem/paradise-lost-book-i-lines-221-270.

"History consists...of the miseries brought upon the world by pride, ambition, avarice, revenge, lust, sedition, hypocrisy, ungoverned zeal and all the train of disorderly appetites which shake the public.... These vices are the cause of the storms. Religion, morals, laws...are the pretext."

The problem today is not that religion permits killing. Many religions allow the use of force, even deadly force. Your life is no less valuable than another's, and if one seeks to extinguish your life, you have an obligation to defend yourself even at the price of his death. We do not have to resort to grand principles—common sense will do—to recognize the difference between murder and self-defense. The well-worn phrase, "One man's terrorist is another man's freedom fighter," is, at its core, a cynical, even nihilistic view of the world. It is simply not true. There is right and wrong, good and evil, life and death, even if locating what is right, good, and life affirming is often a complicated and uneven process.

The problem is not that religion permits killing, but it is the misplaced emphasis on killing. We speak too much of aggression, murder, terrorism, jihad, and extremism, and not enough about the sanctity of life.

Jewish tradition looked at Cain's murder of his brother Abel in an effort to understand the rippling effects of murder. These were the first human brothers, the only brothers alive at the time. They both offered sacrifice to God, but only Abel's offering was accepted. Thereupon, Cain set upon his brother and killed him. God admonished Cain: *What have you done? Your brother's blood cries out to Me from the ground.* Jewish sages noticed that in the original Hebrew, the word for "blood" is written in the plural—literally—*the voice of the bloods of your brother cry out to Me.* In explaining why the word for "blood" is written in the plural, the rabbis wrote that when Cain murdered Abel, he killed not only one man; he also killed all of the future generations that should have descended from this man. In effect, God said to Cain, "You have murdered all of your brother's children—the future lives who will never be born because of you." These are the voices that are crying out to God.

We do not speak enough about peace. Violence, bloodshed, and killing are concessions, not the ideal. *I will banish the bow, sword, and war from the land.* The Bible was careful to point out that David, the greatest of the warrior kings of Israel and progenitor of the messiah himself, was prevented from building the Jerusalem Temple because he had blood on his hands. The House of God could not be built by the man of war.

Religion emphasizes the power of the spirit more than the power of the sword. *Not by might, nor by power, but by My spirit, said the Lord of Hosts.* Moses was denied entrance into the Promised Land because he struck the rock rather than speaking to it. Jewish sages explained that in this one act of striking the rock, Moses introduced religious coercion into the world. He invoked God not through gentle words but through force. He shifted religious discourse from speaking to striking, from persuasion to coercion. Religion seeks to convince, not coerce. Spiritual understanding comes through reflection, not rage. The role of religious leaders is to transform the rod from an instrument of force into an instrument of fealty.

We are much too angry today. *Anger dwells in the bosom of fools.* We do not speak gently enough. *Give up anger, abandon fury, do not be vexed; it can only do harm.* We are not pleasant enough in our presentation of religion. *Its ways are ways of pleasantness and all its paths are peace.* The Talmud clarifies that a religious person, especially if he is a religious leader, is obliged to behave pleasantly because he personifies for others the presence of God on earth. Religious leaders should behave in such a manner that others will say of them: "See how pleasant are their ways!"

We do not emphasize enough mercy and forgiveness. *Mercy and truth are met together in God.* "The quality of mercy is not strained./ It droppeth as the gentle rain from heaven…. It is an attribute to God Himself;/ And earthly power doth then show likest God's/ When mercy seasons justice."[11]

※ ※ ※

I regret not getting to know better my neighbor, Mario. We would meet casually from time to time in the elevator. He was thirty-two years old. He was gentle and kind, entirely different from the stereotypes of the so-called masters of the universe working on the top floors of the World Trade Center who presumably cared only about their financial portfolios. He had an infectious smile, full of humanity. He made it to the upper floors of American society, but he did not forget his humble origins. He was the first of his family to go to college. I later

---

11   William Shakespeare, *The Merchant of Venice*, 4.1.190-203, https://shakespeare.folger.edu/shakespeares-works/the-merchant-of-venice/act-4-scene-1/.

read in the newspaper that Mario planned to leave Wall Street in seven years so that he could use the money he made to give back to society. We never really know these things about each other until it is too late. We discover them the day after, never the day before.

Sometimes mail addressed to Mario arrives in our building. The last piece was from Fidelity Investments. Mario must still be on their mailing list. It was, I would imagine, just boilerplate information, something about a recent change in investment strategy. I picked up the envelope, stared at Mario's name, and reflected on what was lost. Had he lived, whatever investment Mario had at Fidelity would have increased substantially. Even more, Mario's human capital would have compounded exponentially. That is what we really lost on that day. Imagining all the people he would have met, befriended, and loved; the new lives that would have issued from him, the good he would have done for the benefit of humanity—it brought tears to my eyes. When Mario died, these investments ceased, his portfolio terminated before its time.

Two days after 9/11, I walked out of my apartment to find a man who was standing at the entrance to the building. I did not ask his name; I wish I had asked, because I have thought about him for years. He appeared troubled. He had a vacant and distant look about him that was broken only when his son, a toddler in a stroller, mumbled some thoughts or gestured in some way. I was not worried or perturbed. All of us were shocked and dazed. The city was filled with people who were walking around as if in a trance, looking for something or someone. I assumed that this man was probably one of those street walkers. I asked him if he was looking for anyone. He said that he worked with Mario and was with him as they began walking down from the eighty-fourth floor of the World Trade Center. He heard that Mario never came out, and he felt a need to visit Mario's apartment. He wanted to be around him, to feel his essence. He thought that he might run into Mario's parents, and he wanted them to know how highly people regarded their son. I have a feeling that somewhere within him he was hoping beyond hope that Mario had somehow survived and simply returned home. I had that hope too; that Mario would just walk out the door, that it was all some misunderstanding; that he really was alive and, like so many of us, walked up Third Avenue that night and went to bed.

The man told me what had happened on that day. Mario was with him as they began walking down the burning building. The difference between death and life, between demise and survival, was so trivial, that to this day, I am unable to grasp the full enormity of the banality. Mario decided to stop at the restroom on the way down. He told his office mates to continue without him, and he would catch up with them. That was the difference between life and death; the extra time that it took Mario to visit the bathroom. I have never overcome my sense of injury or offense. Why was the life of this gentle soul snuffed out because of something as stupid as stopping for a minute or two?

What have these murderers wrought? Mario would have had children. He would have brought happiness to all those fortunate enough to have come his way. Decades of life were ahead of him. The blood of the innocent cry out from Ground

Zero: "You murdered this man—but not only that: You murdered all of the lives that would have issued from this man. You have extinguished entire worlds. You are your brother's keeper. What have you done?"

I showed Mario's colleague the missing person flyer that his family had posted at the entrance to the building. He burst into tears. It was not a melancholy weeping. It came from a deeper place. It was inconsolable sadness. The man's son, who looked to me to be about two years old, probably a bit confused and shaken at the sight of his weeping father, reached up from the stroller and grabbed his father's arm. I remember thinking: here was the beginning of healing—life and death; optimism and despair; finality and a new beginning in the form of a small child's outstretched little hand. We will survive. Life will go on. We will rebuild our shattered lives and our broken city.

I think about that boy often. He is in his twenties now. I hope that he is living a good life. I hope that he is doing all of the things that young men should do. I hope that he is happy. I hope that his father is still alive and well. The difference between having a father and not having a father is the time it takes to stop at the restroom. I hope that this boy I saw two days after 9/11 lives a long, meaningful, and useful life. I hope that he dedicates himself to something good. I hope that his father told him about Mario; not to depress him, but to the contrary, to inspire him.

In the end, Mario's story is our story. It is a story of hope. It is a story of self-improvement and social repair. It is a story of those who refuse to descend into the pits of despair. It is a story of rebuilding and recommitting. It is a story of those who look for the good in people and who climb ever higher, striving toward the light.

How sweet is the light and how pleasing to the eyes to see the sun!

It is a story of breaking out and breaking away, above the clouds that darken our lives, as we ascend the ladder to heaven.

Lords of Literalism

God is in heaven and you are on earth,
therefore, let your words be few.

(Ecclesiastes 5:1)

Religion preaches the reality of God while insisting that we can never fully understand God. Our powers are limited. God is omnipotent. Our knowledge is partial. God is omniscient. We are mortal. God is immortal. We are of this world. God is beyond this world. We conceive of God exclusively in human terms, but God is not human. We describe God, but God is ineffable. We approach God, but God is unapproachable. We seek God, but God is hidden. We aspire to do God's will, but God is not fully comprehensible to us.

We can never span the chasm that separates us from God. Even Moses, the only human who spoke with God face to face, was incapable of comprehending God beyond his limited human capacities. On the peak of Mount Sinai, Moses asked, "How shall I describe you?"

I will be who I will be, God responds.

Speaking about God, describing God's attributes, requires humility. *This man, Moses, was a humble man, more so than any other man on earth.* The higher Moses climbed toward God, the more humble he became. The more he knew, the more he knew how little he really knew. The closer he came to God, the greater was his distance from God. The most beautiful minds realize that the more knowledge they acquire, the more humble they should be. It is like stalks of wheat, wrote Michel de Montaigne: They rise high, erect and proud as long as they are empty. But when the stalks are full—swollen with grain— in their ripeness they grow humble and lower their horns.

Theology requires intellectual modesty. "Why is the Torah likened to water?" asked the Talmud. "It is to teach you that just as water flows from a higher level to a lower level, so too, the words of Torah only flow [from on high] to the one who is humble."

Even fundamentalists, those who claim that the Bible is the literal record of God's intentions, concede that human beings interpret the Bible. Therefore, even by the standards of the most literal-minded believers, religion is, at least, a partially human endeavor. Human beings make mistakes all the time. Is it conceivable that we would make mistakes in every aspect of our lives but not in the task of interpreting the Bible?

A classic Jewish comment imagines Moses writing the Torah on Mount Sinai. When he came to a verse that he thought might give rise to a heretical understanding, he turned to God and said, "Master of the Universe, why do you give heretics an opportunity [an opening to claim heretical assertions]?" God responded, "Write, and whoever wants to read wrongly will read wrongly." People are going to make mistakes. They are going to read texts wrongly. It is impossible to shield the sacred texts from error. We bring our entire human arsenal with us to the task of interpretation—our intellectual strengths, but also our prejudices, predispositions, and fallibilities. God preferred that people make mistakes, and even proclaim heresies, rather than insist on one interpretation pronounced by one infallible interpreter.

It is not only a matter of making mistakes. People are different; they analyze words and events differently. As secular judges give different interpretations of legislative intent, so too do religious judges give different interpretations of divine intent. "Why was the Torah given in the wilderness?" asked one Jewish commentary. "Just as the wilderness has no limit, so the words of the Torah have no limit." One casual glance at the world reveals the truth of this assertion. Within any given religion, there are different and competing perspectives of the same sacred texts. Judaism and Christianity parted ways, not because of different bibles. What Jews call "Tanakh" and Christians call "The Old Testament" are essentially the same: the difference is in the interpretation.

Jewish tradition emphasized that every person understood the Law differently at Mount Sinai. They heard the same words but understood them in their own particular way. "God speaks to each and every person differently, according to his particular capacity; just as a hammer strikes the rock and it shatters into many pieces, so does a single verse [of Torah] yield many meanings."

We should revel in our differences. Diversity is a good thing. Pluralism is the bedrock of freedom, and freedom is religion's central assumption and most insistent demand.

Centralization—the impulse toward uniformity—is the mindset of Pharaoh. This mindset objectifies human beings and leads to totalitarianism and dictatorship.

Anything human is uncertain. Religion too. To be human is to be uncertain. We will never know the answers to the big questions of life. We cannot say with certainty what our lives will be like tomorrow. If we do not even know whether we will be alive tomorrow, why do some think they can say with certainty how everlasting life will look? We take a leap of faith. We believe. It is why we describe religion as "faith," and religious people as "believers." To believe is also a form of knowledge. It is insight, intuition, imagination, feeling—and intellect and logic too—but it is not certainty. There are no absolutes in life and no certainties. We must make our peace with not knowing everything, especially as it relates to the unknowable God.

Fundamentalists often hurl this accusation: "We are certain of good and bad, right and wrong, morality and immorality; the rest of you are simply a bunch of moral relativists."

This, of course, is nonsense.

Fundamentalists, too, are selective; they select the most literal and the most restrictive of many possible interpretations. But a literal approach is only one way to interpret the Bible. Who said that it is even the best or most sophisticated way? Lords of literalism often overestimate their own capacities and underestimate the timelessness and expansiveness of the sacred texts.

Morality lies not only in the original articulation of a biblical mandate, but in its application to continually changing circumstances. The Bible is a living document only if it continues to evolve. For example, dozens of biblical verses describe clearly and in detail methods of capital punishment, yet Jewish law has, for all intents and purposes, prohibited capital punishment. Half the Orthodox Jewish world eats rice on Passover and half does not. Both believe they are faithfully implementing Jewish law, and both have followed the same methodologies, but have reached different conclusions—one more restrictive and one less restrictive. Is one school definitely right and another definitely wrong? Perhaps. We shall know for sure when the Messiah arrives, but in the meantime, why not admit that both approaches can be authentic and simply lead to different outcomes?

In the heavens there are absolutes, not on earth. Human beings cannot live with each other on the basis of absolutes. There is a passage in Jewish tradition that describes a debate between God and the ministering angels immediately before the creation of humanity. When God was about to create Adam, the angels formed two groups. Love and Righteousness urged God to create human beings. "They will be capable of, and will do, acts of love and righteousness," the angels insisted. Peace and Truth urged God not to create human beings because they "will commit acts of war and falsehood." The angels were split evenly on whether to create Man. What did God do? He took Truth and cast it to the ground. The vote was then two to one in favor of creating Adam, and thus Man was born.

Absolute truth cannot exist in a human setting. There are no absolutes in life. Everything is filtered through human understanding and human emotion, and thus subject to the basic human condition of imperfection. Some are convinced that there is only one way to interpret the Bible—their way; only one way to worship God—their way; only one way to enforce God's will—their way.

Why do we insist on only one interpretation in religious matters, when in so many other human endeavors we encourage plurality? Is there only one way to read a poem? Is there only one way to produce Shakespeare? Is there only one way to play Beethoven? Did Beethoven even intend his sonatas to be interpreted in only one way? Is there only one way to understand a masterwork? If human poets insist that there are multiple ways to understand their poetry, why insist that there is only one way to understand God's poetry? If a human masterwork can be analyzed from many perspectives, why analyze God's masterwork from only one perspective? Why would God have created each of us unique, different from each other, if He intended only one understanding, one way and one approach? How can a faith live; how can values mature, if one understanding is fixed for all time?

By whose authority do some people insist that there is one fixed understanding of sacred texts for all time? Certainly not by God's authority. We read in the Talmud how Moses—who tradition regards as having received the word of God directly—was transported many centuries ahead into the academy of the venerated sage Akiva, who was lecturing about Jewish law. Moses sat in the back row and tried to follow the discussion, but to no avail. During the lesson, one of the students asked Akiva how he knew that his interpretation of a law was the proper one. Akiva answered that it was given to Moses at Sinai. Moses, however, could not understand Akiva's reasoning, nor could he even remember having received this interpretation from God. Nonetheless, it was a valid and authoritative interpretation.

If you claim to know with certainty the will of the Almighty One, you tend to be impatient with those who do not see the light as you do. You will describe people who hold differing views as enemies. You will ascribe to them indecent motives. You will prescribe extreme remedies for their impudence. Impatience leads to intolerance. Intolerance leads to extremism. Extremism leads to violence. Violence leads to evil. Isaiah Berlin wrote:

> One belief, more than any other, is responsible for the slaughter of individuals on the altars of the great historical ideals…. This is the belief that somewhere, in the past or in the future, in divine revelation or in the mind of an individual thinker, in the pronouncements of history or science, or in the single heart of an uncorrupted good man, there is a final solution.

Most of us have read about or met people who are convinced that they have found the final solution. These sellers of certainty are convinced that God endowed them with a perfect understanding of the divine will, revealed to them, alone. In the eyes of those who know everything about God, the rest of us are not merely mistaken, we are sinners. Why else would we persist in challenging their (perfect) comprehension of God's will?

They see in every challenge an affront to God. They interpret every doubt as an insult to God. They convince themselves that they are God's protectors and defenders. They are quick to take offense. They are quick to mete out justice. Churchill wrote that a fanatic is a person who won't change his mind and won't change the subject. Religious fanatics cannot be persuaded because they are beyond reason. They are overzealous. They are supercharged. They won't change their minds, and they won't change the subject. It seems that there is no lightness of being in them. They lack any subtlety or sense of humor. They seem incapable of self-reflection. They spend too much time contemplating heavenly rewards and not enough time focusing on earthly travails. Sometimes you just want to say to them, "Relax, don't get so uptight. God is not so easily offended and does not need your angry defense or zealous prosecution."

Why are those most certain about what God wants so often the ones who seem most ready to violate God's commands? Those who are most adamant about defending God's honor are often the ones with the fewest qualms about committing atrocities. They serve up a false religion. The seemingly noble traits of devotion, piety, honor, and dignity ferment in the heart of the zealous and become intoxicating. Error, ignorance, superstition, hatred, and prejudice mix together in the human heart to produce an evil brew.

Why is it that God speaks most clearly to those who are most extreme, leaving the rest of us in the dark about His true intentions? Why are the most fanatical among us the loudest?

Words spoken softly by wise men are heeded sooner than those shouted by a lord in folly.

We read in the Book of Job:

Who is this who speak[s] without knowledge? Where were you when I laid the earth's foundations? Speak if you have understanding. Do you know who fixed its dimensions? Have you ever commanded the day to break? Have the gates of death been disclosed to you. If you know of these—tell Me. Who is wise enough to give an account of the heavens?

There are people who can memorize every word of sacred texts and who have encyclopedic knowledge of every interpretation and every citation. What good is such knowledge if there is no understanding? Religion's goal is to instill goodness. Its ultimate aim is to bring about peace. The Talmud writes: "What is said of someone who studies Torah…but does not deal honorably and does not speak pleasantly with people? Woe to that person who studied Torah. Woe to his father who taught him Torah. Woe to his teacher who taught him Torah.'"

Crusades have been launched to defend God's honor; holy warriors dispatched to protect God's dignity. The service of God usurps God. "'Tis mad idolatry," Shakespeare wrote, "to make the service greater than the god." "I beseech you, in the bowels of Christ, think it possible that you may be mistaken," pleaded Oliver Cromwell to the General Assembly of the Church of Scotland before the campaign in Scotland. Their response could have been written today: "Would you have us to be skeptics in our religion?"

Given the state of the world today, a dose of humility would go a long way. The Talmud states: "Teach your tongue to say, 'I don't know,' lest you be exposed as a liar." *I am but dust and ashes*, said Job. How then could we be in possession of absolute truth? The very assertion is blasphemous. Only one who does not understand the religious mindset considers doubt an indictment of religion. Doubt is not the enemy of faith. Doubt is what gives faith meaning.

In religious matters, it is best to follow the advice of Rabbi Menachem Mendel Morgensztern, commonly known as the Kotzker Rebbe:

"Take care of your own soul and another person's body, rather than your body and another's soul."

On Miracles

*He performed marvels in the land of Egypt. He split
the sea and took them through it. He made the waters
stand like a wall. He led them with a cloud by day,
and throughout the night by the light of fire. He split
rocks in the wilderness and gave them drink...*

(Psalm 78:12-16)

*Do not imagine that you, of all the Jews, will escape
with your life. On the contrary, if you keep silent in
this crisis, relief and deliverance will come to the Jews
from another quarter, while you and your father's
house will perish. Who knows, perhaps you have
attained this royal position for just such a crisis.*

(Esther 4:13-14)

The Bible offers two models of salvation. The first is the
exodus from Egypt. God controls practically everything. God manipulates Pharaoh, hardening his heart.
God manipulates nature, bringing the ten plagues. God splits
the sea. God destroys the Egyptians. God reveals Himself at
Mount Sinai amid thunder, lightning, and divine fireworks.
You cannot miss the presence of God. The Israelites had little
to do with the great deliverance. Moses would have failed had

God not performed miracles and marvels. God wanted deliverance to occur in this way. God was prepared to do the heavy lifting, and the people bowed to His brute force:

> *Go to Pharaoh, for I have hardened his heart and the hearts of his courtiers so that I may display My signs among them—and that you may recount how I made a mockery of the Egyptians, and how I displayed My signs among them—in order that you may know that I am the Lord.*

The second model of salvation is described in the Book of Esther. Here, God is silent. The name of God is never mentioned in the ten chapters of the scroll. Redemption is dependent upon human action. God operates, not as the overwhelming force crashing in from the outside, but as an inner light, a beacon, inspiring human beings to manifest God's purpose. Naturally, every character in the Esther story is flawed. They are human. Nonetheless, limited and flawed human beings bring about the deliverance.

The Sages recognized the historical evolution from the redemption of Egypt to salvation in Persia. In one of the most brilliant passages in all of Jewish literature, the Talmud links these two models of deliverance. We read that when the Israelites arrived at the foot of Mount Sinai, God overturned the mountain and threatened to bring it crashing down on the Israelites if they declined to accept the Torah. Sensing that this type of coercion cannot constitute a true covenant between God and the Jewish people, the Talmud quickly adds, "Even so, they reaffirmed the covenant during the time of Achashverosh," the king of Persia in the book of Esther.

Why reaffirm the covenant at all? It was already sealed at Sinai. Moreover, even if it needed additional reaffirmation, why during the time of Esther, when God was silent?

Miracles are a form of manipulation. If once a day, we were to witness an impossible event—say, a house elevating fifty feet above ground, violating the laws of gravity—we might come to believe. However, it would not be a free belief, because we would have been manipulated into believing. For this reason, the signs and wonders of Egypt were unsustainable in the long run. The high of miracles wears off quickly. Miracles are shallow—the ancient equivalent of a quick fix. God had to overcome centuries of silence, so the drama had to be impressive. One can hardly think of a more impressive sequence of events than the step-by-step miraculous dismantling of the world's ancient superpower, Egypt, and the humiliation of the taskmasters and their all-powerful Pharaoh. If ever you were to believe, this would be the time. But even before God hardened Pharaoh's heart, he quickly changed his mind after each plague. Pharaoh's conversion lasted only for a short moment.

Life is about the daily struggle for survival. Miracles are fine, but you still need to put food on the table. The fix wears off quickly. The Israelites started complaining only three days after the splitting of the Red Sea. It didn't take long for disbelief, rebelliousness, and apostasy to set in. And therefore, the conquest of the Promised Land could not take place immediately. It took forty years of wandering in the desert for the Israelites to understand deeply and to know deeply. The Sages emphasized that the long wilderness experience was necessary so that knowledge of God would be absorbed into the bloodstream of the Israelites—that it would "settle in their bodies"—and so that they would be refined, as metal is refined and purified. There were no quick fixes to belief. It was, at most, a forty-day trek from Egypt to the Promised Land. It should not have taken forty years. But in the end, there could be no shortcuts. Miracles could not replace the mundane. Knowledge of God required slow understanding. All the miracles of Egypt could not short-circuit four decades of contemplation.

Over time, some Jewish thinkers came to understand miracles not as a supernatural occurrence, but an unexpected one. We might describe the recovery of a patient who survives a fatal disease, contrary to all known medical science, as a miracle. What we mean is not a supernatural intervention that upended the laws of nature, but a recovery so astoundingly unexpected as to render it incomprehensively astonishing in our eyes.

Faith has never been dependent on miracles. Quite the contrary, to claim or expect miracles as the main ingredient of faith is to compromise faith. Explaining the baffling reluctance of the Israelites to put their faith in Moses, Maimonides wrote that "when someone's faith is founded on miraculous signs, there is always lingering doubt that these signs may have been performed with magic or witchcraft."

The Talmud advises: "One should never put oneself in a dangerous situation and say, 'A miracle will save me.' Perhaps the miracle will not come. And even if a miracle occurs, one's merits are reduced."

Exodus is the book of miracles. But if we look at the total arc of the Bible and subsequent Jewish tradition, we may conclude that Judaism's approach to history assumes that as the eras unfold, miracles of obvious divine intervention—sound and light and thunder, plagues, seas parting—these become less prominent, and human deeds become more prominent. The Bible tells us that the manna stopped falling from heaven the day the Israelites first ate of the produce of the Promised Land. The era of the Exodus was over. From now on, they would need to produce their own food.

One of the central prayers of the High Holy Days is *Unetaneh Tokef*. We recite it only on Rosh Hashanah and Yom Kippur. There is a phrase in the *Unetaneh Tokef* that always moves me:

Ve'kol d'mama daka yishama—a still small voice is heard.

That phrase—*kol d'mama daka*—is taken from the Book of Kings, describing the prophet Elijah. He was fleeing the idolatrous King Ahab and his wife Jezebel. He found a cave and hid inside. He was all alone. He was in despair—perhaps the lowest point of his life—and he asked God to die: "Enough," he cried, "take my life."

"Come out of the cave," God commanded, "and stand on the mountaintop." And then we read:

"And lo, the Eternal passed by and a great and strong wind split the mountains and shattered the rocks— but God was not in the wind.

After the wind, an earthquake—but God was not in the earthquake.

After the earthquake—a fire—but God was not in the fire.

After the fire—*kol d'mama daka*—a still small voice."

After the Exodus era, God is perceived not through bombast, noise, earthquakes, wind, and fire, but through softer, more subtle, more sophisticated signs.

James Russell Lowell wrote this magnificent poem, "A Parable":

Worn and footsore was the Prophet,
When he gained the holy hill;
'God has left the earth,' he murmured,
'Here his presence lingers still.

'God of all the olden prophets,
Wilt thou speak with men no more?
Have I not as truly served thee
As thy chosen ones of yore?

'Hear me, guider of my fathers
Lo! A humble heart is mine;
By thy mercy I beseech thee
Grant thy servant but a sign!'

Bowing then his head, he listened
For an answer to his prayer;
No loud burst of thunder followed,
Not a murmur stirred the air:

But the tuft of moss before him
Opened while he waited yet,
And, from out the rock's hard bosom,
Sprang a tender violet.

'God! I thank thee,' said the Prophet;
'Hard of heart and blind was I,
Looking to the holy mountain
For the gift of prophecy.

'Still thou speakest with thy children
Freely as in eld sublime;
Humbleness, and love, and patience,
Still give empire over time.

'Had I trusted in my nature,
And had faith in lowly things,
Thou thyself wouldst then have sought me.
And set free my spirit's wings.

'But I looked for signs and wonders,
That o'er men should give me sway;
Thirsting to be more than mortal,
I was even less than clay.

'Ere I entered on my journey,
As I girt my loins to start,
Ran to me my little daughter,
The beloved of my heart;

'In her hand she held a flower,
Like to this as like may be,
Which, beside my very threshold,
She had plucked and brought to me.'[12]

---

12   James Russell Lowell, "A Parable," AllPoetry.com, https://allpoetry.
com/poem/8546749-A-Parable-by-James-Russell-Lowell.

Between Two Worlds

Before the mountains came into being, before
You brought forth the earth and the world,
from eternity to eternity You are God.

(Psalms 90:2)

Ancient Greece must have been magical.
To wander the streets of Athens is a mystical experience. Giants walked these hills. Pericles was here. I stood where he stood. I can see him giving the speeches that stirred Athenians: words still studied by speechmakers. The vividness of the image astonishes me. I hear him. I can almost touch him. What I would give to study oratory with the master.

Athens overflows with antiquities. Everywhere, there are reminders of ancient days. There by the modern park is a Roman bath. By the shop on the side street are first-century mosaics. By the museum, an ancient neighborhood. By the Acropolis, an ancient village. These are antiquities for us, but twenty-five hundred years ago, the Acropolis was not ancient. It was new. The Athenians did not consider themselves "Ancient" Greeks. They were Greeks. They lived for the day. We know them, but they did not know us. They built the

Parthenon, not so that two and a half millennia later a tourist from New York could trek up the mountain. They did it for themselves, not us. They wanted to honor the goddess Athena. Ruins move me. A few rocks, a wall, and a pillar from antiquity are enough to seize my imagination. I felt so alive walking the streets of the dead. I created an entire world in my mind: how the ancient Athenians looked, how they worked, how they dressed, how they dined, how they talked. It is a bit voyeuristic. We peek into the lives of those who lived thousands of years before without them knowing that we are looking in. It is like reality television. Our imagination replaces the hidden cameras.

That is the fascination of ruins: Ruins renew. Ruins restore. Ruins remind that we are not alone. We are part of a continuum. There was life before us. There will be life after us. The past shapes us. We are who we are because they were who they were. In this way, ruins recompense, reimbursement for the brevity of life and reparation for its finality. Ruins respond to our unrequited hunger for meaning and immortality, redeeming the dead, easing our feelings of fleetingness.

People die. It is the law. Pericles died. Socrates died. Hippocrates died. Thucydides died. The strong and the weak, the mighty and the meek; as Shakespeare put it best in Hamlet, "All that lives must die, passing through nature to eternity." Buildings crumble. Pillars fall. The temples collapse. The mightiest civilizations gone with the wind.

It is all so humbling. Gazing at the dust of Ancient Greece, one of our species' most remarkable achievements, I was moved by how moved I was. Here at my feet lay the spokes of the great wheel of life. What an awesome thought: We are not alone. We are in the bloodstream of human existence.

At the Acropolis, I saw a Japanese family that had carried an elder up the hill in a wheelchair. They struggled to push the chair over the rocky terrain. It was hot. Thousands of people were on the mountain. Unperturbed, they clanked laboriously from one temple to another. Why the effort, I asked myself. Just see the movie. But seeing the movie won't cut it. You have to be here: to feel the heartbeat of history and the pulse of solidarity that binds all who ever lived; a Japanese woman from the East, an American man from the West, and everyone in-between.

Tourists at the Acropolis behaved as tourists do. They were noisy, they trampled on ancient artifacts, they thought mostly of themselves, snapping selfies in the sanctuaries of the gods. Still, I would like to believe that they paid all that money and invested all that effort to lug themselves up the mountain for one faint feeling of liberation: Life is bigger than myself and my selfie. Democracy, philosophy, medicine, theater, so much of Western civilization was born here. I am part of all that I have met. I am inside the flow of time, a participant, a player, not a passerby.

Ancient ruins take us back as far as we can see, but the past is billions of years older. History is only the last part; the human part, the seam of recognizable time we desperately hold onto like a fragile thread. We view the Acropolis as ancient, but it is less than three thousand years old. The Ancient Greeks could not even see that far back.

One day, we will be the Ancient Americans. One day, if there is anything left, tourists will visit where we live now: "Here lay the remnants of ancient New York." They will peer over the excavated remains of Grand Central Station and imagine how we looked, how we worked, how we dressed, how we dined, how we talked: how we moved—trains will be a thing of the past.

And like the Greeks of old, we Americans of the 21st century will constitute only the very last part, the human part, of the past. If humanity survives, our era will merge with all the eras, one time of many times. And even if humanity does not survive, time is eternal and will continue with or without us. We are an imperceptible speck on the space-time continuum. Our three score year and ten, or perhaps four or five score years, are as nothing.

We are finite, but all around us is infinity. The universe is too big for us. The microscopic, too small. Telescopes are ever more powerful, but we are mostly blind to what lies beyond. Microscopes are ever more powerful, but we are mostly dumb to what lies inside.

We are unable to see the beginning or the end. We have come a long way. We are making great strides. What we know is remarkable. What we will know is inconceivable. But let no one deceive or pretend. Physicists see practically nothing of what there is to see. Chemists see practically nothing. Software developers see practically nothing. Historians see practically nothing. Politicians see practically nothing. Mental health experts see practically nothing. Self-help masters see practically nothing. Rabbis see practically nothing. Some human beings think they know more than they do; and they tell us what they think they know with considerable confidence, but they know practically nothing of what there is to know. They see hardly at all.

The truly brilliant of our species acknowledged and embraced our limitations. Einstein wrote: "The most beautiful emotion we can experience is the mysterious…. To sense that beyond anything that can be experienced there is something that our minds cannot grasp, whose beauty and sublimity reach us only indirectly."

We live between two worlds, the world of the past and the world of the future. The past is infinite. The future is infinite. We live between two infinites.

HANDPRINT UNDER
SOLOMON'S TEMPLE

In the 480th year after the Israelites left the
land of Egypt...in the fourth year of his reign...
Solomon began to build the House of the
Lord. It took him seven years to build it.

(I Kings 6:1, 38)

Israeli archeologists are digging to the very foundations
of the Jewish people. Some of their finds are spectacular.
Others are prosaic. All are important. Slowly, but inexorably, the bedrock of our people's history is revealed.

The hardest layer to get to is the First Temple period. It
is the oldest, and hence, the deepest underground. Moreover,
the Al-Aqsa Mosque sits on the spot where both the First and
Second Temples stood. Moving even one fistful of dirt under
the mosque could cause the Middle East to explode. Thus,
artifacts from the First Temple period are extremely rare—
not because they do not exist, but because they cannot be
reached. Third-millennium politics of the Common Era prevent discovering first-millennium treasures from Before the
Common Era.

Still, now and again, something amazing emerges. Some years ago, while digging under the Western Wall, a floor began to give way. Eventually, part of it collapsed, revealing a massive underground reservoir. Archeologists could hardly contain their excitement. The reservoir dated from the First Temple period. Still visible were the remnants of the yellow plaster commonly applied during those times. Water from winter rains would run downhill from the Temple Mount and seep into this reservoir, filling it to capacity. At the time of the summer dig, after six rainless months, there was still a pool of fresh water left there from the winter rains. The best thinking now is that the reservoir was a plentiful source of water for the public to use around the Temple for drinking, bathing, and ritual purposes.

As moving as all this is, the most fascinating find was that the handprint of a laborer who added the yellow plaster was still visible on the wall. I imagine those laborers plastering. I can see them in my mind's eye. I can smell their sweat and hear their banter. It was a job for them, but for me, they were not simply among the countless people who lived uneventful lives and lay in forgotten tombs. They are us. They are me. In some way that we cannot fully fathom or articulate, we are the products of those who came before. These laborers left their mark on us. They built Jerusalem. One of them left behind not only the water reservoir he sweated over, but something much more personal: his handprint, a physical sign of his presence.

It would be as if 3,000 years from now, sometime around the fifty-first century, someone would stumble upon the fruit of my labors. I am not a construction worker, but perhaps they might discover some memo or sermon that would allow them to draw a direct connection to me, even if they never figured out that it was I who actually wrote that document.

This is a form of immortality, the only kind available to creatures of flesh and blood. Immortality is in the memory of others; in the fruits of our labor that we leave behind. Immortality is when someone in the future—a century from now, a millennium from now—discovers something of us. They may not even know our name. But when they see what we produced and think about it, when they utter an idea that we spoke, we live. Our era lives in them. Our lives counted. We meant something. We paved the road to the future. In this way, time, that is such an efficient destroyer—it causes decay, it covers up and obliterates what used to be—can also reconstruct. When we discover a handprint of a laborer under Solomon's Temple, our identity is refortified and rebuilt.

We will never know the laborer's name, but his memory remains. His essence is in me. The moment I look at what someone left behind, whether the words of Shakespeare or a laborer's handprint, I feel his feelings. I dream his dreams. He lives in me. Immortality is not corporeal, but spiritual: ideas, words that set the imagination to flight. A handprint on a wall deep underground, perhaps left there intentionally, reminds us that we are part of something larger than ourselves. We are part of the human race. We are part of the Jewish people, whose founders thought of us at the founding moment. They dreamed of us. They built for us. They struggled, endured, created, and died for us.

The Bible states that it took seven years to complete the First Temple. Jewish lore describes how King Solomon would go in disguise to examine the progress of the construction. He met with three workers and asked each what they were doing.

The first said to him: "I am tanning the ram skins."

The second said: "I am crushing the olives to make oil that will light the menorah."

The third said: "I am working on the place where the people will meet God."

Solomon praised the third worker alone. Only he truly understood the meaning of the work. The laborers were making a living. They served the king. But one of them left his handprint to help us imagine the place where the people met God.

Three thousand years later, this handprint helps us to envision our own meeting with God.

II.

THE JEWS

The Angel of History

I will not wholly wipe out the House of Jacob.

(Amos 9:8)

In early 1940, Walter Benjamin, the brilliant German Jewish thinker, wrote what would be his final essay. It contained these words:

> A Klee painting...shows an angel.... His eyes are staring, his mouth is open, his wings are spread. This is how one pictures the angel of history. His face is turned toward the past. Where we perceive a chain of events, he sees one single catastrophe which keeps piling wreckage and hurls it in front of his feet. The angel would like to stay, awaken the dead, and make whole what has been smashed. But a storm is blowing in from Paradise; it has got caught in his wings with such violence that the angel can no longer close them. This storm irresistibly propels him into the future to which his back is turned, while the pile of debris before him grows skyward. The storm is what we call progress.

The Angel of History can only face the past. Even as he is propelled toward the future, he cannot see it. He cannot turn around; he cannot close his wings; the storm prevents it. He can only see what has already transpired. And he sees not what we would see—a chain of historical events—one event after another. The angel sees only one single catastrophe. History for him is wreckage and destruction. He would at least like to change the past: to stay a while; to awaken the dead and to make whole what has been smashed. But alas, this, too, is beyond him. He is powerless in the face of the storm. The storm comes from Paradise itself. It has been raging since the beginning of time. It is what we call progress.

If I were to hitch a ride on the angel's wing and embark on a fantasy flight back to Jewish history, the angel would point not to a series of events, but to one single catastrophe that, in the name of progress, keeps piling Jewish wreckage upon Jewish wreckage ever skyward, the debris reaching the gates of heaven itself. But not being an angel, I would want to see a series of events.

I would want to see Egypt; to stop for a while and to witness the deliverance with my own eyes: to feel the birth pangs of freedom, when oppression was discredited for all time. "Wait, slow down; there is Moses in the palace of the Pharaoh. Did you hear that? 'Let my people go!'" I would like to view below the great Day of the Lord: the humbling of the taskmaster, slavery's sea split, and the glorious birth of a people sworn to uphold liberty, dignity, and justice for all time. "Wait, slow down, there is Moses descending from the mountain with the two tablets of stone, carved into the very foundations of Western thought. There is Joshua crossing the River Jordan. There is David and his son, Solomon; and there, on Mount Moriah, is the Temple."

What a magnificent time to be alive: emancipation and deliverance.

But we would be propelled quickly forward by the storm blowing from Paradise, I on the wing of the Angel of History. History is only catastrophe, he would say. In the blink of an eye, he would show me destruction: the disintegration of the Northern Kingdom of Israel, the destruction of the Temple, exile, and a pile of debris growing skyward, to the gates of heaven itself. "Wait: at least let us go down and stay for a while; to awaken the dead and make whole what was smashed."

But alas, the storm from Paradise keeps blowing, and we are hurled into the future. It is what we call progress.

I would like to stop and see the return of the exiles from Babylon, but the Angel of History cannot stop. Down below, the reconstruction of the Temple would whiz by. How glorious! The renewal of sovereignty, the rejuvenation of the Jewish state, the return of the Jews and the rebuilding of God's home in the City of Peace.

What a magnificent time to be alive: emancipation and deliverance.

But we would be propelled quickly forward by the storm blowing from Paradise, I on the wing of the Angel of History. History is only catastrophe, he would say. In the blink of an eye, he would show me destruction: destruction of the Second Temple, exile, and a pile of debris growing skyward, to the gates of heaven itself. "Wait: At least let us go down and stay for a while, to awaken the dead and make whole what was smashed."

But alas, the storm from Paradise keeps blowing, and we are hurled into the future. It is what we call progress.

I would like to stop and meet the rabbis, inventors of the Talmud, the saviors of Judaism. I would like to study at the feet of Akiva, argue with Rabbi Ammi, whose name I bear, and witness the triumph of hope over despair. I would like to swill French wine with Rashi, intoxicated by the brilliance of his commentary. I would like to philosophize with Maimonides in Spain; to travel the highways and byways of Europe; to visit the Sephardic towns of the Mediterranean basin; to overnight in the hundreds of thriving Jewish communities that rebuilt Jewish life in exile.

What a magnificent time to be alive: emancipation and deliverance.

But we would be propelled quickly forward by the storm blowing from Paradise, I on the wing of the Angel of History. History is only catastrophe, he would say. In the blink of an eye, he would show me destruction: pogroms, persecutions, blood libels, fires raging in the shtetls, wholesale religiously inspired murder; a pile of debris growing skyward to the gates of heaven itself. "Wait: At least let us go down and stay for a while; to awaken the dead and make whole what was smashed."

But alas, the storm from Paradise keeps blowing, and we are hurled into the future. It is what we call progress.

I would like to stop and meet the Jews of the Enlightenment: to dine in their fine homes; to watch as they helped invent modern science, composed beautiful music, wrote great literature, cured disease, and financed, with their entrepreneurial talents, so much of the renaissance of Europe.

What a magnificent time to be alive: emancipation and deliverance.

But we would be propelled quickly forward by the storm blowing from Paradise, I on the wing of the Angel of History. History is only catastrophe, he would say. In the blink of an eye, he would show me destruction: the burning of what they called Jewish science, Jewish art, Jewish music, Jewish morals, Jewish philosophy, and eventually, the burning of the Jews themselves. The Angel of History would show me the ghettos, the railways, the furnaces, the chimneys, the ovens, the mass shootings: A pile of debris growing skyward to the gates of heaven itself. "Wait: At least let us go down and stay for a while; to awaken the dead and make whole what was smashed."

But alas, the storm from Paradise keeps blowing, and we are hurled into the future. It is what we call progress.

And so, my flight ends. The Angel of History has deposited me back where I started. What a magnificent time to be alive: emancipation and deliverance. Many of us live in the Golden Land, most of the rest of us in the Promised Land. While the Angel of History sees only one single catastrophe, we see another glorious age upon us.

We have done what Jews have always done: we have scratched and crawled our way up from the deepest valleys of destruction to the ascendant heights of deliverance. Always life-affirming, always looking up; there are always better days ahead. Mindful of the wholesale destruction of the last century and the blood-curdling threats of this century, we have risen from the ashes. It is what we call progress. For Jews, history is not the history of wreckage. For us, history is the history of recovery from wreckage.

What enormous forces of will were implanted within us that we could rise time after time? Jewish tradition teaches: "On the day that Jerusalem was destroyed, the Messiah was born." It is a stunning and distinctively Jewish idea: the seeds of Jewish revival are planted in the soil of destruction, lying in the wreckage, waiting to be nourished and to sprout again.

To take a flight on the wings of the Angel of History is to realize that even the greatest civilizations thrived for but a moment in time. Once knocked down, they could not get up. The distinctive attribute of the Jews is not that we were knocked down, but that we got up when others could not. We should not be here. Our existence is contrary to the laws of history. Believers are left to ponder: for some unfathomable reason, God ordained the survival of the remnant of this people: *You will keep faith with Jacob, loyalty to Abraham, as You promised on oath to our fathers in days gone by.*

Walter Benjamin died on September 27, 1940, at the age of forty-eight. After the fall of Paris, Benjamin made his way south. The only escape route was by foot, through the Pyrenees, into Catalonia, Spain, and from there, a train to Lisbon, where he would board a ship to the United States that had already granted him a visa.

In eastern France, he hooked up with Lisa Fittko, who would eventually shepherd hundreds of refugees over the mountains. On September 26, Benjamin, Fittko, and two other refugees reached the summit of the Pyrenees. Below, at their feet, lay freedom—the fishing village of Portbou, Spain. Fittko returned to France and the escape party made their way down into the village.

It was an arduous journey for Benjamin. He had a heart condition and had to rest every ten minutes. His companions feared that he would die on the mountain. He insisted on lugging a heavy suitcase with him, scratching, crawling, falling, dragging it up every narrow path. Lisa Fittko later described how Benjamin would not part from the suitcase. He said that it contained a valuable manuscript, some major new work that he had been laboring over for years. "This briefcase is the most important thing I have. I mustn't lose it," said Benjamin. "My manuscript must be saved. It is more important than I am." Benjamin believed that the ideas of a man outlast the life of a man.

When the refugees arrived in Portbou, Spanish authorities refused to grant them safe passage and threatened to return them to France. Benjamin felt that this meant certain death. He no longer had the strength to evade the Nazis. He had stayed one step ahead of them since fleeing Berlin in 1932. Consistent with his nature, he had meticulously planned for this eventuality. He packed enough morphine, said his friend, Arthur Koestler, to kill a horse. The next morning, September 27, Walter Benjamin, one of the most lucid, brilliant, and beautiful minds of the 20th century, was dead, having taken the fatal overdose sometime during the previous night.

The suitcase was never found. Many have searched for it through the years. Perhaps it is lying in some basement or attic, gathering dust, waiting to be discovered. Perhaps it was destroyed. Perhaps it is simply lost forever.

I am fascinated by the missing suitcase. What was inside? What penetrating insight about life and history had this gentle genius produced? He felt that his manuscript was even more important than his own life, but the great tragedy of the death of Walter Benjamin is that both his life and his final manuscript were lost on that night in late September. When he took his life, he took his manuscript with him.

It is comforting for me to imagine that the Angel of History has the suitcase: that the storm blowing from Paradise ceased for a moment, imperceptible to us, but not to the angel. And at that very instant of calm, he flitted in, late in the night of September 26, 1940, and grabbed the manuscript for safekeeping as its creator slowly drifted away.

Since the manuscript in the suitcase is lost to us, we are left with these final words in the final published work of Walter Benjamin:

> We know that the Jews were prohibited from investigating the future. The Torah and prayers instruct them in remembrance, however. This stripped the future of its magic, to which all those succumb who turn to the soothsayers of enlightenment. This does not imply, however, that for the Jews the future turned into homogenous, empty time. For every second of time was the strait gate through which the Messiah might enter.

Every second of our time on earth might be the straits through which the Messiah might enter. We are limited creatures. We live in the narrow straits of earthly time; we do not see the whole picture. We see only fragments and fractions. But every second of our time might be the moment through which messianic time may trickle in. This is what Jewish tradition teaches. Walter Benjamin got that right. Every moment is pregnant with potential and possibility.

Never give up; never despair. Get up! Rise and rise again, from one catastrophe to the next, and continue to climb toward the heights, lugging your suitcase of questions and your manuscript of meaning with you.

We may never reach the top, but our labor is not in vain. The ascent is our way to understand the world. We awaken the dead and make whole what was smashed. To choose life is to give life to those who came before. We validate their lives by finding purpose in our lives. The Torah and prayers instruct us that our actions can make a difference. Our aim is to break open the narrow straits of history: to vest history with meaning and our lives with purpose. Evil can be vanquished and good can reign.

And at that moment, when the narrow straits of our time are penetrated by messianic time, the storm from Paradise will break. Our days will be calm. The Angel of History can finally rest. All creation will be at peace.

THE OTHER TWO TABLETS

How can I give you up, O Ephraim,
how surrender you O Israel?

(Hosea 11:8)

There is a ten-foot stone slab in the Egyptian Museum in Cairo. Commonly known as the Merneptah Stone, it describes the military victories of the pharaoh, Merneptah, the fourth ruler of the 19th dynasty. Carved approximately in 1200 BCE, it contains history's first known reference to the Jewish people. For this reason, some call it "The Israel Stone." Peeling away 3,200 years of civilization, we can peek into the very origins of Jewish life. The pharaoh mentions us only in passing, just one short phrase. We were almost an afterthought. Still, there we unmistakably are. The seed of Israel is sprouting.

What did the king say about us? That we were nice? That we were strong; that we were smart; that we were hard workers; that we were rebellious; that we were funny; that we had many neuroses; that we liked lox and bagels? What were the first words ever written about the Jewish people? At the bottom of the slab, recording the deeds of the "lord of strength whose name is given to eternity," as Merneptah described himself, he wrote:

"Israel is laid waste, its seed is destroyed."

"I destroyed the Jews." This is history's first ever mention of the Jews.

There is a black basalt stone slab in the Louvre in Paris. Commonly known as the Mesha Stone, it describes the military victory of Mesha, the Moabite king, over Omri, the king of Israel, around the year 850 BCE. Outside of the Bible, itself, this is history's second-known mention of the Jewish people.

What did Mesha write about us? That we were strong; that we were smart; that we were hard workers; that we were rebellious; that we were funny; that we had many neuroses; that we liked lox and bagels? What was the content of the second-ever reference to the Jews?

"Israel is lost forever," wrote Mesha, 350 years after Merneptah forever destroyed us the first time.

History's first two references to the Jews boast of our extinction. What is it about the Jews that prompts so many rulers to seek our destruction? Their claims of extinction are always premature. *The life of a mortal man is of numbered days, but the life of Israel is of days without number.*

What sprightly corpses! The living descendants of the left-for-dead nation meander the halls of the Cairo museum, where they gaze at the works of the long-dead Merneptah, pharaoh of the long-extinct Egyptian Empire. They stroll the Near Eastern Antiquities Department of the Louvre, where they view the tablet of the long-dead Mesha, king of the long-lost Moabites.

Then they move on to the Mona Lisa....

Natan-Melech

*And King Josiah took away the horses that the
kings of Judah had previously given to the sun at
the entrance to the House of the Lord and Josiah
burned the chariots of the sun with fire by the
chamber of his officer—Nathan-Melech.*

(II Kings 23:11)

J osiah was one of the greatest and most consequential of the
Israelite kings. In the eighteenth year of his reign, around
the year 622 BCE, he purged the Jerusalem Temple of
the idolatrous practices of his predecessors. There must have
been some kind of ancient foreign ritual of dedicating horses
and chariots to the sun. The Israelites were so corrupt by the
time of King Josiah that the priests themselves performed this
idol worship at the very entrance to the Temple, the House of
God. Josiah took away these horses and burned the chariots.
This took place by the chamber of one Natan-Melech, an officer of the king.

Hardly anyone ever gave any thought to Natan-Melech.
He is mentioned only once in the Bible, and only in passing.
The point of the eleventh verse of the twenty-third chapter of
II Kings is not to tell us about Natan-Melech, but to locate

where King Josiah burned the idolatrous chariots. It was by the chamber of his servant, Natan-Melech, who must have been such a prominent public official that everyone knew where he lived. To say "by the chamber of Natan-Melech" would have been enough for the ancient reader or listener to know precisely the location in Jerusalem. It would be like saying today, "I'll meet you by the mayor's house," or, "The parade passed by the Empire State Building."

Over 2,600 years later, that man, Natan-Melech, has vaulted back from near-obscurity and thrust into the very heartbeat of Jewish history. Natan-Melech has come alive, back from the long dead. Israeli archeologists recently discovered an ancient seal impression with his name. The size of a fingernail or two, the tiny clay tablet used in antiquity to seal documents was imprinted with ancient Hebrew letters spelling:

L'Natan-Melech Eved Ha'Melech—"Belonging to Natan-Melech—Servant of the King."

It must have been him—the same Natan-Melech mentioned in the Book of Kings.

I stared and stared at the pictures of the ancient seal. Natan-Melech might have personally held this seal in the palm of his hand. Millennia ago, one of our Jewish ancestors imprinted the letters and baked the clay in a kiln. And someone—Natan-Melech or, perhaps, his staff—fastened documents with it. Our ancestors walking the ancient streets of Jerusalem carried parchments sealed with this tiny clay bulla bearing the name of Natan-Melech.

It was found inside the ruins of a massive building where a very wealthy Jerusalemite must have lived. Charred remains of wooden beams were discovered inside the house. Israeli archaeologists tell us that these are the remains of the fires set by the Babylonians in the year 586 BCE that destroyed the First Temple. And there, inside that home, this tiny seal was discovered by the charred wood. It survived because it was made of hardened clay.

Natan-Melech spoke in the name of one of the pivotal leaders in all of Jewish history, Josiah, king of Israel. Scholars tell us that Judaism might not have even survived were it not for Josiah, who, they speculate, found or wrote some version of the Book of Deuteronomy, the last of the Five Books of Moses. We were well on the way to oblivion, like all the other nations of antiquity that were conquered by Egypt, Assyria, Babylonia, Persia, Greece, and Rome, the superpowers of the ancient world. Josiah rebelled. Josiah fought back. Josiah restored the Temple. Josiah either discovered or wrote Deuteronomy. Without Josiah, would we even be here?

And Natan-Melech was one of his officers who helped the king save Judaism in its infancy. Therefore, even though Natan-Melech was mentioned only once in the Bible, in passing, he was a critical figure because he was a high-ranking official of the indispensable king. And his seal was found by 21st century explorers of the Bible.

It is overwhelming. This tiny object, buried in the earth for more than 2,500 years, and waiting to be discovered one day—this small seal of an almost-forgotten Jerusalem official—links two extraordinarily monumental moments in

Jewish life: First, King Josiah, the indispensable leader whose reign affected Judaism to this day. Second, the destruction of the First Temple by the Babylonians less than twenty-five years after Josiah died in war. It was one of the most dramatic events in all of Jewish history. To this day, Jews still mourn the loss of the First Temple.

I can see it all. I can recreate everything in my imagination. Josiah, Natan-Melech, the idolatrous priests—Jerusalem— they are all alive in me.

Natan-Melech lived. Natan-Melech lives now. All you have to do is imagine him. You can see his seal and picture how he looked, how he spoke, what he said. And by imagining him, you can reimagine yourself. Since Jerusalem is slowly revealing its buried secrets, it is easier to bridge the millennia and trace our lives to the source, the wellsprings of Jewish life. We would not be here if they were not there. Without the Jews of yesteryear, there would be no Jews today.

The past shapes us. We are in the bloodstream of Jewish existence.

THE ARCH OF TITUS

You shall make a lampstand of pure gold. Six
branches shall issue from its side; three branches from
one side and three branches from the other side.

(Exodus 25:31-32)

In excavating the Western Wall of the Jerusalem Temple, Israeli archeologists uncovered huge boulders lying in front of the Southern Wall of the Temple complex known as Robinson's Arch. They thought of clearing them to make room for tourists, until they realized that these were the very boulders heaved down upon the Jews from the burning Temple Mount by Roman soldiers as they sacked and burned the Temple. Ancient soot from millennia-old fires still blackens the boulders. If you touch them, you touch one of the saddest, most tragic episodes of our people's past. If these boulders could recount what they saw, they would tell of the pillaging, looting, and killing of the Jews; the sheer panic and chaos; the violence, the blood that ran like water in the gutters of the Holy City.

Josephus, the former Jewish commander who surrendered to the Romans and joined them in the siege of Jerusalem, described it this way:

[Roman soldiers] went in numbers into the lanes of the city, with their swords drawn, they slew those whom they overtook, without mercy, and set fire to the houses wither the Jews were fled, and burnt every soul in them, and laid waste a great many of the rest; and when they were come to the houses to plunder them, they found in them entire families of dead men, and the upper rooms full of dead corpses…[that] obstructed the very lanes with their dead bodies, and made the whole city run down with blood, to such a degree indeed that the fire of the many houses was quenched with these men's blood.

Titus was the Roman general who sacked Jerusalem. In 69 CE, he assumed supreme command of the Roman legion from his father, Vespasian, who returned to Rome and became Emperor after Nero's death. Vespasian struck the heavy blows against the Jews. Titus delivered the coup de grace. They printed coins honoring Vespasian's victories. You can still see those coins in museums.

To honor Titus, they commissioned a victory arch. We know it today as the Arch of Titus. You can still walk through it if you cross the street from the Coliseum and proceed for several hundred meters through the Forum. On the bottom corner of the Arch of Titus is a frieze depicting Roman soldiers carrying the Temple's Menorah—the seven-branch candelabra. Titus's frieze is the ancient equivalent of a photo or film, documenting that the last known resting place of the Temple Menorah was Rome.

The Menorah was magnificent. The Bible states that it was made of pure gold. Scholars tell us that pure gold is the highest grade, having undergone extra steps in the refining process to free it from any impurity. Pure gold symbolizes the Jewish dream of refinement and purity. The Menorah was symbolic of our ambition to create a more peaceful world, a world filled with light. Ultimately, the Menorah became the symbol of Jewish sovereignty. The emblem of the modern State of Israel is the Temple Menorah. By carrying the Menorah back to Rome, the Romans were announcing the end of Jewish sovereignty. The Jews would soon disappear from the pages of history like all the other nations that the Romans subjugated and defeated. The Romans were convinced of that.

In the year 71, Emperor Vespasian arranged a victory march in Rome to honor his son and to parade in front of the Roman people the spoils of war. Josephus, who moved to Rome after the destruction and become the chronicler of the Jewish War, described the scene with this firsthand eyewitness account:

> Notice was given in advance of the day appointed for the victory procession, and not one person stayed at home out of the immense population of the City. Everyone came out, and although there was only standing room, they all found a place somewhere, so that there was barely enough room left for the procession itself to pass.... Vespasian and Titus came out wreathed with bay and wearing the traditional crimson robes.... A dais had been set up in front of the colonnades, and on it placed ready for them

were ivory chairs. On these they proceeded to sit; whereupon the soldiery shouted acclamations, one and all, bearing full testimony to their prowess…

It is impossible to give a satisfactory account of the innumerable spectacles, so magnificent in every way one could think of, whether as works of art or varieties of wealth or rarities of nature… Masses of silver and gold and ivory in every shape known to the craftsman's art could be seen, not as if carried in procession but like a flowing river. Numbers of tableaux showed the successive stages of the war most vividly portrayed. Here was to be seen a smiling countryside laid waste, there whole formations of the enemy put to the sword—men in flight and men led off to captivity—great strongholds stormed, cities—whose battlements were lined with defenders—utterly overwhelmed…. Such were the agonies to which the Jews condemned themselves when they embarked upon this war….

Most of the spoils that were carried were heaped up indiscriminately, but more prominent than all the rest were those captured in the Temple in Jerusalem: A golden table weighing several hundred weight, and a lamp stand similarly made of gold…. The central shaft was fixed to a base, and from it extended slender branches placed like the prongs of a trident, and with the end of each one forged into a lamp. These numbered seven, signifying the honor paid to that number by the Jews….

The procession finished at the Temple of Jupiter on the Capitol, where they came to a halt; it was an ancient custom to wait there till news came that the commander-in-chief of the enemy was dead. This was Simon, son of Gioras, who had been marching in the procession among the prisoners, and now with a noose thrown round him was being dragged to the usual spot in the Forum while his escort knocked him about. That is the spot laid down by the law of Rome for the execution of those condemned to death for their misdeeds. When the news of his end arrived it was received with universal acclamation and the sacrifices were begun…. Sumptuous banquets had been prepared…. All day long the city of Rome celebrated the triumphant issue of the campaign against the [Jews].

When the triumphal ceremonies were over, Vespasian made up his mind to build a temple…. He adorned it with paintings and statues…. He laid up the golden vessels from the Temple of the Jews—for he prided himself on them.

That was it: the end of the line for this people. It was good while it lasted, but nothing lasts forever. The kingdom survived for a thousand years, from Saul to Shimon bar Giora, one of the three commanders of Jerusalem during the siege. The Menorah, the very symbol of Jewish independence and self-determination, was in bondage at its holding site—what the Romans perversely called the Temple of Peace. The Temple of Peace was funded through the plunder brought back from the war on the Jews. One wall of that Temple still stands in the Forum. But the Temple of Peace, along with ancient Rome itself, is dust and rubble.

The Jewish people live on. The Menorah has been rekindled in Jerusalem. It burns eternally. It is the Romans who are no more. If only Vespasian, if only Titus, could see the Eternal People, the nation they could not destroy, back in the Land of Zion and Jerusalem.

They must be rolling in their graves.

By the Home of Rudolf Höss

A new king arose over Egypt who did not know Joseph,
and he said to his people: "Look, the people of Israel are
much too numerous for us. Let us deal shrewdly with
them so that they may not increase, otherwise, in the
event of war, they may join our enemies and fight against
us. So they set taskmasters over them to oppress them...

(Exodus 1:8-11)

To visit Auschwitz is to enter the mind of Pharaoh. Pharaoh decreed the first attempted genocide of the Jewish people. Hitler was his student. Ignoring the centuries-long contributions that Jews made to Germany, Hitler warned, "Look, the Jews are much too numerous for us. In the event of war, they will join our enemies and fight against us." So they set taskmasters over the Jews to oppress them.

Rudolf Höss, the commandant of Auschwitz, was the chief executioner. He became the most prolific mass murderer in the history of humanity. Höss oversaw a new way to kill: modern mechanized mass murder. In prison after the war, he wrote, with pride, about the technology of death that he administered. He considered it a great achievement, an outstanding professional accomplishment. Apparently, Höss never murdered any of the prisoners with his own hand. He was not the brutal sadist that we often imagine when thinking of Nazis. By all accounts, he was an attentive family man. He loved his five children and they loved him. He took the time to spend weekends and afternoons on family outings. At the edge of the camp stands a locked gate, beyond which is the Höss family home. The mansion abuts Auschwitz. The contrast is incomprehensible. On this side is evil, torture, suffering, slavery, cruelty, and depravity. Over the fence—a football field away, within the grasp of your hand—is freedom and normalcy, tranquility, a happy family, an attentive father, a loving mother, laughter, gaiety, joy: hearth and home. The ability of the human creature to be good and evil, humane and barbaric, at the same time in the same person, our ability to cordon off atrocity, preventing the stench from invading our happy corner—these are mysteries of the highest order.

Höss lived with his family within eyeshot of the gas chamber. Hedwig, his wife, testified that these years were the best and most comfortable years of their lives. Höss made no attempt to move his family away. To the contrary, even after he was promoted and transferred to Berlin, he kept his family in the mansion. They didn't want to move to Berlin since their lives were so comfortable at Auschwitz. The children later described how their mother insisted they wash the strawberries they picked in the garden because they were covered with dust. It was the dust of murdered human beings.

We are able to tolerate in ourselves sharp contrasts and rationalize inexcusable contradictions: tranquility for my family on the grounds of Auschwitz. A family man who thought nothing of annihilating millions of other families. It is not that some of us are mostly good and some of us are mostly bad. It is that within all of us is good and bad. Höss was a human being, not some kind of fictional monster with sub-human or super-human attributes. It is why he was so terrifying. He was human. If he did it, if he thought it, it is proof that these are within the realm of human possibility. What human beings have done once, they can do again. All are capable of atrocities. We can never trust ourselves completely. We cannot devise institutions that are so secure, so hermetically sealed, that they will stop rampant moral pollution.

Rudolf Höss did not conform with our stereotype of a genocidal murderer. Nor did many Nazis who devised and executed the annihilation of the Jews. The Final Solution was planned at Wansee, a lakeside villa outside Berlin. Half the participants of the Wansee conference carried the title "doctor." They were educated. They were cultured. At one in the same, they were refined and savage. In our technological age, refined savages are the most dangerous of all.

From inside the camp, behind the locked gate, I noticed movement on the grounds of the Höss mansion. There was a car in the backyard. The garden was manicured. The house looked lived-in. There was a family living there! A normal family—living by the gates of Hell—in the monster's mansion—undeterred by the history of the place or even the two million visitors a year who probe the depths and mysteries of human depravity emanating from their house. I was told that the current occupants consider this a Polish house. The Nazis expelled the family that lived there, and Höss moved his family in. After the war, that original family reclaimed their home, eventually selling the property to the ancestors of the current occupants. It is a Polish house, they say, not a Nazi house. A normal family lives in the most abnormal place. They can find peace and quiet in a house haunted by the ghosts of the terrorized. The current residents may be good people—I hope they are. Perhaps they sympathize with the Jews and all those murdered at their doorstep eight decades ago. My point is not to cast judgment on the family, or to suggest that the younger generations are personally responsible for the sins of their parents and grandparents. Rather, it is to highlight how easily human beings can distance themselves from the suffering of others. A family lives in the mansion of history's most notorious mass murderer. They lead uneventful lives on the grounds of Auschwitz.

In the end, life moves on. Many thousands of people visit Auschwitz every day, desperately trying to make sense of the barbaric cruelty unleashed here. But the people who live right outside live normal lives. They have families. They raise children. They have pets and satellite television. Our dismay is not their dismay. Our disquiet is not their disquiet. Our tragedy is not their tragedy. They do not recoil from the stench of Auschwitz quite the same way.

As I gazed over the fence from inside the concentration camp grounds, trying to imagine the lives of the current residents living in the Höss mansion, I remember thinking to myself: No one feels your pain as you do. No one feels your peril as you do. If you suffered calamity, no one is as committed to "Never Again" as you are.

I have limited patience for those who accuse Jews of being too sensitive to blood-curdling threats leveled at us. After all we have been through, centuries of hatred, oppression, persecution, genocide, violence, and discrimination, we have a right, even a responsibility, to take threats of extermination seriously. If another catastrophe were to befall the Jewish people: if, for example, Iran were to drop one nuclear bomb on Tel Aviv—all that is needed to destroy Israel, according to the ayatollahs—there would be blazing headlines. Learned books would be published. Millions would express real and sincere sadness. Some would weep. A few might repent. But in the end, they would move on. We would be left with the tragedy.

To this day, two thousand years later, Jews mourn the destruction of the ancient Jewish state. For everyone else, it is a small piece of history, if they are even aware of it. For us, after two millennia, it is still an open wound. It will never fully heal.

Never again: it is, first and foremost, a Jewish responsibility.

A Synagogue in Bratislava

And they shall make for me a sanctuary,
that I will dwell among them.

(Exodus 25:8)

Bratislava once contained a thriving Jewish community. On the eve of World War II, Jews were 12 percent of the population of the city. Today, there are an estimated 800 Jews left. As you drive to the center of the old part of town, you see from the main road a stunning large yellow Moorish synagogue—testament to the revitalization of Jewish life decimated by the Nazis. The synagogue is in the heart of the town square adjacent to a magnificent church. How heartwarming—a church and a synagogue standing side by side in harmony—symbolizing the possibilities of coexistence between these ancient sister faiths.

As you drive closer to the synagogue, you begin to develop a gnawing feeling that something is not right. It is hard to pinpoint. The church next door looks old and weather-beaten, but the synagogue sparkles. Its colors are vibrant. It looks as if it survived the 20th century's upheavals in perfect shape.

Upon disembarking from the bus, you realize what is off with this scene. The synagogue is fake. It is a true-to-life model. It looks real from the road, but it was constructed recently, in order to remind people of the grandeur of what used to be, not of what is. It is nothing but a few planks of wood and yellow drapery. It is like a movie set, a fantasy synagogue. It is not living. It is dead. There is no sanctuary for God to dwell in.

This is what the final spasms of Jewish life look like. There are still some Jewish remnants in Europe. Mostly, though, Europe is one giant Jewish graveyard. The tragic truth is that Hitler largely succeeded in his insane pathology to rid Europe of Jews. What Hitler did not finish, Stalin did. These are the final hours of Jewish life in much of Europe. A once vital and vigorous Jewish community, on its knees, crawling through the Valley of the Shadow of Death.

Why did they build this fake synagogue? To encourage foreign Jewish travelers to stop in Bratislava for an afternoon and spend a little money? To promote religious coexistence? To assuage the guilt of modern-day Slovakians, some of whose ancestors aided and abetted the decimation of the Bratislava Jewish community and no doubt worshipped in the neighboring church?

To walk through the fake synagogue is to remember that European Jewry was annihilated not only because of Man's inhumanity to Man, but also because of Man's inhumanity to Jews. We were the target of their insane murderous rage. Many other people suffered, and many others were killed. Jews do not have a monopoly on suffering. But it was only our people that was marked for murder simply for being. That is what made the Holocaust unique in the annals of human civilization. There was no way to escape the decree. From the moment of birth, we were singled out for death.

The fake synagogue reminded me of the museum to the extinct race that Hitler planned for Prague. Hitler envisioned a mountain of Jewish artifacts from throughout Europe permanently exhibited in one of his favorite cities. The Nazis did not mind collecting the stuff of dead Jews. They did not want the memory of the Jews extinguished from Europe. They wanted living Jews extinguished from Europe. They largely succeeded.

Is the fake synagogue in Bratislava a gesture of respect? Remorse? Is it a museum to the once great and now practically extinct Jewish community of Slovakia?

PAVEL

These words which I command you this day shall
be upon your heart. Teach them diligently to your
children, talk of them when you are at home and on
the way, when you lie down and when you rise up.

(Deuteronomy 6:6-7)

When I first met Pavel Stransky in Prague, he was ninety-one years old. He was slight, perhaps a few inches over five feet. His short half-beard had turned white long ago. His face was radiant. His eyes were undimmed, his vigor unabated. On rainy days, he walked with an umbrella in place of a cane, but his mind was still clear as a bell.

Pavel accompanied us to Theresienstadt, the infamous concentration camp in the Czech city of Terezin, where tens of thousands of Jews died, and where many tens of thousands were transported to Auschwitz and Treblinka.

Theresienstadt was a uniquely ghoulish place, even by Nazi standards. It was not an extermination camp, but a prison, where the Germans concentrated Czech Jews for eventual transportation to death camps. They used Theresienstadt for propaganda, making films purporting to show the world how well they treated Jewish prisoners. Many world-class Jewish artists, authors, and musicians were imprisoned there, leaving behind a moving and tragic collection of paintings, drawings, and compositions. There was even an orchestra in the camp. Brundibar, the children's opera, was performed in Theresienstadt.

When Pavel was seventeen, he fell in love with Vera, who was sixteen. It was love at first sight, he said. In 1941, they were both deported to Terezin.

In December of 1943, Pavel learned that he would be transported to the East. Thousands died in Terezin of punishment, disease, and malnutrition; but Pavel said that as bad as conditions were, it was luxury compared with Auschwitz. The night before the deportation, he married Vera. They couldn't bear to be parted, and the only way they could stay together was if they married. No one knew that their destination was Auschwitz, or that the Germans had constructed extermination camps to execute their final solution to the Jewish problem. "The day before my departure, we got married," he said. "And our honeymoon was Birkenau. Had Dante seen the ramp in Auschwitz-Birkenau at the end of the night of December 20, 1943, he would have been ashamed of his sober description of Hell."

Pavel's job in Auschwitz was to distract, and keep busy, children who were about to be sent to the gas chambers. He told me that Josef Mengele, the infamous Nazi doctor who was in charge of the selections, would visit his barracks every Wednesday. "Did you speak with him?" I asked.

"No, never," said Pavel. "You couldn't speak to the commanders of the camp. It could mean death."

"What was Mengele like?" I asked.

Pavel responded, "He was the kind of man who could play with the children, laugh with them, bounce them on his knee, tell them to call him 'uncle,' and send them to the gas chambers the next day."

Pavel survived Auschwitz and an inhuman death march, and eventually ended up back in Theresienstadt when the Soviets liberated the camp. He began the Holocaust in Terezin and he ended the Holocaust in Terezin. Ultimately, he made his way back home to Prague, a drive of about an hour. "The happiest day of my life," he said, "was two months later: the doorbell rang, and standing in front of me was my Vera. She was a real beauty." He showed me her picture. Somehow, she, too, survived Auschwitz.

Pavel then described how he and Vera resumed their love affair. They carried on, living long and meaningful lives. Vera died in her seventies, Pavel in his nineties. They did everything a couple is supposed to do in life. They laughed, they learned, they rejoiced, they grew old together. They had children. They had grandchildren. Even though Pavel lost Vera fifteen years before we met, it was evident that he still loved her deeply and thought of her every day, many times a day. "We lived through a happy marriage without any single stormy cloud in its sky, with beloved and loving children," said Pavel. "And later on, we included their wives into these relations, and still, later on, of course, our grandchildren. All of them returned us our love and do so now to me."

Pavel then turned to me and said, "My grandchildren are not Jewish."

The more you study the Holocaust, the more elusive are the answers. The more you learn, the less you know. The harder you try to explain, the more inexplicable it is. I understand—and have no quarrel with—those who walked out of the camps and could not reconcile a Jewish future with their past sufferings imposed upon them simply for being Jewish. I understand those who could never again believe in a God who abandoned them at the Gates of Hell.

Besides, I felt so much love for Pavel, for his courage, his dignity, his humanity; for his strength, his quiet determined demeanor undiminished after all these years. Pavel survived and prevailed. He defeated Hitler. He rebuilt his life under the hardships and depravations of the Communist regime. He was productive. He was accomplished. He lived to see the third generation of Stranskys bouncing on his knee.

In the many years since I met Pavel, his matter-of-fact emotionless statement to me that he and Vera had no Jewish grandchildren stuck with me. I had not pried it out of him. He volunteered the information. Perhaps in the final years of his life, walking the grounds of Theresienstadt as he had dozens of times before with similar groups, he simply took the opportunity to share his thoughts with a rabbi. I never asked him whether he was bothered that his family's long chain of Jewish transmission ended with Vera and him. Some Jews walked out of the camp and were determined to repopulate the Jewish world, no matter what. Others swore that they would never again speak of Judaism or impose on their families the curse of Jewishness. I do not know what Pavel's intentions were when he and Vera began raising a family. Sometimes, life just unfolds, irrespective of, or despite, our intentions.

In the Bible, as Jacob is about to die in the Egyptian Diaspora, he called his favorite son, Joseph, to his side, intent on blessing Joseph's two children. Joseph presented the boys to his father. Despite having lived with these grandchildren for many years, Jacob looked at them and uttered a remarkable phrase—one of the most baffling verses in the Bible.

Who are these kids? he asked.

According to one interpretation, Jacob did not recognize his own grandchildren because he peered into their future and saw a future of alienation, an abandonment of Jewish civilization. At that moment, Jacob panicked and asked, "Who are they? I can't recognize them?" According to the medieval commentator Rashi, it is only after Joseph showed Jacob his ketubah, the Jewish marriage license, symbolizing Joseph's intention to raise his children with a Jewish heritage, that Jacob recognized them and blessed them.

Irrespective of the personal decisions Holocaust survivors made for themselves and their families, there can be only one response to the Holocaust for the Jewish people:

To produce a third generation, not only of good people, but good Jewish people.

Not only a third generation, but a third generation of Jews.

III.

ISRAEL

THE PROMISED LAND

I will restore My people Israel. They shall
rebuild ruined cities and inhabit them;

They shall plant vineyards and drink their wine;

They shall till gardens and eat their fruits.

And I will plant them upon their soil, nevermore
to be uprooted from the soil I have given them.

(Amos 9:8, 14-15)

I often recite these verses to myself on the plane, upon first glance of the Tel Aviv skyline, as the white city slowly rises from the azure sea. The return of the Jews to Zion is a miracle of biblical proportions. Our people have raised Zion from desolation and made it live again. *The song of the turtledove is heard throughout the land. The green figs weigh heavy on the fig trees, the vines in blossom give off fragrance. The mountains drip with wine, and the hills wave with grain.* The prophecy has come true! Israeli cities teem with energy. Its wines are among the finest in the world. Dozens of countries use Israeli technology to till gardens and grow food in unforgiving climates.

Israel embodies the Jewish people's indomitable will to survive. We endured centuries of persecution, oppression, hatred, mass murder, and wholesale annihilation of entire communities. We should have disappeared long ago.

It is a miracle that there are even Jews in the world. There are no Babylonians in Brooklyn, Philistines in Phoenix, Moabites in Montana, Midianites in Mississippi, or Canaanites in Colorado. I have never met an Amalekite, a Hittite, an Akkadian, a Sumerian, a Chaldean, a Hyksos, or a Nabatean. None of the nations of antiquity mentioned in the Bible, often cited as seeking our destruction, survived. The passing centuries consumed even the superpowers of the ancient world, their crumbling ruins displaying scant reminders that they once dominated their times.

The State of Israel is a triumph of the human spirit. Tortured on the crosses of the inquisition, bleeding on the steppes of the Pale, incinerated in the furnaces of Europe, despised and discriminated against in the lands of the crescent—a nation left for dead a thousand times—revived.

As such, the Jewish state has universal significance. Israel represents hope, testifying to the resilience and the grandeur of the human creature. The very existence of a Jewish state says to the world: if the Jews can do it, after all that the Jews have endured, then others can lift up the banner of freedom and restore themselves. Israel is the engine of the recreation and restoration of the national home and the national vigor of the Jewish people: A nation uprooted and scattered to the wind, rehabilitated. A hundred generations passed since the destruction of the Jerusalem Temple, but we never abandoned the dream: *I will put My breath in you and you shall live again, and I will set you upon your own soil once again.*

Jewish national existence in the Land of Israel lasted for a thousand years. It birthed the three great faiths of Western civilization. Our determination to return was not a 20th century innovation. The contemporary political movement called Zionism is simply its latest and most successful expression. The dream of national restoration began the day after the Romans destroyed the Jewish kingdom in the year 70 CE. Israel is not compensation for centuries of persecution. Israel is not restitution for the Holocaust. Israel is the realization of the age-old dream of the Jewish people to come home. As Eudora Welty wrote: "a place that ever was lived in is like a fire that never goes out."

For the Jewish people, the dream of a Jewish state in the Land of Israel was like a fire that never went out. Dispersion was an interruption of, not a replacement for, our national existence in the Land of Israel. We never ceased dreaming of return. We never stopped praying for redemption. "Sound the great shofar of freedom; lift up the banner to bring our people home and assemble us from the four corners of the earth."[13] Jewish sovereignty in the Land of Israel has been the cornerstone of Jewish beliefs and the foundation of Jewish history since the birth of our people. It is as old as Judaism itself.

The modern Zionist movement did not create a new dream. It voiced the ancient dream for modern times. "Zionism is a return to Judaism even before there is a return to the Jewish Land," Theodor Herzl said to the delegates of the First Zionist Congress. It was an astonishing insight, a prophecy we now know to be true. Reviving the Jewish nation revived Judaism

---

13 Part of the Shemoneh Esrei Prayer.

itself. It is impossible to envision Judaism today without the State of Israel. Zionism restored the Jewish people to history, propelling us back to the future.

Ruined cities are rebuilt, the people restored, nevermore to be uprooted from the soil of the Promised Land.

SUITE 117

*Pave the highway, rebuild the road, remove all
the obstacles from the road of My people.*

(Isaiah 57:14)

Traveling one summer in Europe, my wife Alison and
I were so lost in time that two days before our return
to the States we found ourselves 400 miles from
Frankfurt, our final destination. Not wanting to drive that
distance in one day, we picked a halfway point for an overnight stopover. We could have chosen many cities, towns, or
villages in several different countries. But since we had never
been to Basel, Switzerland, we thought, "Why not?"

Except for the major tourist destinations, European city
hotels always have room in summer. It is their slow season.
In fact, they usually give summer discounts. So we uploaded
the address of what looked like a good hotel in Basel—Les
Trois Rois—and the GPS guided us there. We arrived mid-af-
ternoon, and sure enough, they had vacancies. They even
upgraded us and offered a summer discount, inviting us to
have a drink on the balcony as they prepared our room.

Les Trois Rois is one of the oldest of the Swiss hotels, established in 1681. It sits on the Rhine. Relaxing on the verandah,

I mentioned to Alison, "Theodor Herzl was here somewhere." The famous picture of him with that far-away gaze overlooking the river must have been taken near where we were sitting. The view was similar. I looked up and down both banks of the Rhine, trying to fathom the precise location. I couldn't visit Basel and ignore the great prophet of Israel, the visionary founder of the Zionist movement, who so influenced my life, many millions of other lives, and history itself. I googled the picture and was stunned: It was shot at Les Trois Rois Hotel, from the balcony of Suite 117—where Herzl stayed during the First Zionist Congress.

A wave of emotion crashed on me. After we settled into our room, I asked the receptionist whether I could see Suite 117. She said she had to check whether the room was occupied. "Wait," I said. "You mean, it is just another room in the hotel, and anyone can stay there?"

"Yes, of course," the woman responded.

"You mean I could have reserved that room?"

"Of course," she said, "but we upgraded you to a better room." I have never been so deflated by an upgrade. That upgrade dragged me down. For me, Suite 117 was the most elevated room in the entire city.

It was unoccupied. The receptionist took us up. My excitement was indescribable. She opened the door. My knees buckled; my eyes moistened. The great man spent several days in this room in late August 1897. I could sense him. I could feel him. The receptionist, seeing my altered emotional state, so different from what she observed five minutes before, must have concluded that I was a history buff because she then said,

"You know, Napoleon stayed at the hotel too." Napoleon? Who cares about Napoleon—that minor historical footnote! I was in Theodor Herzl's room!

The Rhine starts in the Swiss Alps near the Austrian border. There, it is just a puddle formed by melting snow. By the time it reaches Basel, it is at full flow, wide, deep, and strong of current. Looking at the mighty river from the balcony of Suite 117, as Herzl did at the close of the 19th century, I thought what he might have thought on the eve of the First Zionist Congress: the Rhine symbolized the mysterious and ineluctable flow of time. Herzl hoped that those three days would relaunch our listless, demoralized, and persecuted people onto the mighty currents of history, connecting us to the source, the very headwaters of Jewish life—the Land of Israel.

The obstacles were enormous. Zionism was just a trickle. Most Jews were indifferent or opposed. At many points along the way, Herzl voiced despair. "I must frankly admit to myself: I am demoralized," he wrote in his diary. "I feel that I am growing exhausted. Oftener than ever I believe that my movement is at an end. While I am still absolutely convinced of its feasibility, I cannot overcome the initial difficulties." But on August 29, 1897, he was filled with optimism, even rapture: the secular prophet summoned to a kind of religious calling. Receiving a euphoric fifteen-minute standing ovation from the two hundred delegates to the First Zionist Congress, Herzl proclaimed: "We want to lay the foundation stone for the house which will become the refuge of the Jewish nation."

Herzl would be dead seven years after staying in Suite 117, felled at the age of forty-four by a torn heart. But the movement that most Jews rejected on that August week in Basel became the foundation stone for the Jewish nation: *The stone that the builders rejected has become the cornerstone.* The trickle in Basel became a mighty torrent. Herzl gave political voice to our deepest spiritual yearning and most urgent communal need. That was his genius. "Smooth runs the water where the brook is deep."[14] Deep within the mighty currents of Jewish life lay the age-old dream of return. Herzl did not invent this dream, nor was he the first to give it a voice. He was the first to organize the dream politically. That is what made him, a secular Jew of the Enlightenment, who preferred Goethe to Gemara and Hegel to Hosea, one of the most transformative figures in the history of our people.

Herzl engineered the politics of return. He built the architecture of the Zionist movement. At first, the obstacles seemed insurmountable, at times, even to Herzl, himself. But before he died, he had cleared enough rocks, removed enough obstructions, and paved enough roadwork so that his successors could continue cementing the road back to Zion. Many others made vital contributions to segments of the highway, but Herzl was its founding visionary and chief engineer. It is difficult to imagine the eventual establishment of the State of Israel without Herzl.

He must have sensed the possibilities from the balcony of Suite 117. The day after his inaugural speech, he recorded in his diary: "I no longer need to write the history of yesterday: it is already being written by others." On the banks of the

---

14   William Shakespeare, *Henry VI*, 3.1.53, https://www.folger.edu/henry-vi-part-2.

Rhine, our people set sail anew: "There is a tide in the affairs of men, which taken at the flood, leads on to fortune." At the close of the First Zionist Congress, Herzl wrote in his diary: "At Basel I founded the Jewish state. If I said this out loud today, I would be greeted by universal laughter. In five years, and certainly in fifty years, everyone will perceive it."

Fifty years later, in November 1947, the United Nations voted to establish a Jewish state.

In August of the year 70 CE, on the ninth day of the Hebrew month of Av, Roman legions burned the Jerusalem Temple to the ground, bringing to an end a thousand years of Jewish independence. The Jewish sages taught: at the time of the Temple's destruction, young priests gathered on the roof of the sanctuary, with the Temple keys in their hands. As the fires raged below them, the priests proclaimed before God: "Master of the Universe, since we did not merit to be faithful guardians [of your sacred house] we are handing the keys back to You. Thereupon, they threw the keys upward. The Rabbis say that a kind of palm of a hand emerged and caught the keys. The priests then jumped from the roof of the Temple into the fires below.

It took two millennia to restore the House of Israel to the Land of Israel. The determination to self-determination lay unrealized for 1,800 years. It stirred mightily again only at the end of the 19th century, provoked by a renewed explosion of European anti-Semitism, and reenergized by the modern-day prophet who stayed a few nights at Les Trois Rois Hotel. A kind of palm from above dropped the keys into the hands of that remarkable soul who unlocked Suite 117.

He opened the door of the modest, un-upgraded room, laid the bags of two millennia of Jewish history by the bed, went out to the balcony, breathed in the fresh air of modernity, and there, by the mighty river, forever changed the current of Jewish history.

Mount Nebo

*Moses went up from the steppes of Moab to Mount
Nebo...opposite Jericho, and God showed him the entire
land: Gilead as far as Dan; all Naphtali, the land of
Ephraim and Manasseh, the whole land of Judah, as far
as the Western Sea; the Negev and the Plain—the Valley
of Jericho, the city of palm trees. And God said to him,
"This is the land which I swore to Abraham, Isaac and
Jacob, I will assign it to your offspring. I have let you see
it with your own eyes, but you shall not cross there."*

(Deuteronomy 34:1-4)

One of the great spiritual moments of my life was
standing atop Mount Nebo in Jordan. It was one
of those few transformational moments that take
our breath away because they come unexpectedly—out of the
blue—invading our souls without warning or preparation.

In the mid-1990s, I led a group of eighty North American
Reform rabbis on a mission to Egypt, Jordan, and Israel. From
the start, it was an intensely stressful experience for me. I was
the newly installed director of the Association of Reform
Zionists of America (ARZA), young and untested. In representing the North American Reform movement on matters
related to Israel, one of our goals was to help advance peace

between Israel and her neighbors. Egypt had already made peace with Israel in the 1970s. After the Oslo Accords were signed in 1993, talks between Jordan and Israel intensified. Eventually, the two countries would formally make peace in October 1994.

Our mission was to depart in January 1994. It was wildly popular with rabbis. Back then, email was several years from widespread use; we were still in the era of fax machines. Within an hour of sending an announcement, my office fax malfunctioned, such was the rush of colleagues who registered for the mission. We expected to meet with leaders and dignitaries of all three countries and give publicity to their peace-making efforts, thus helping to build public support. In planning the mission, I consulted with the staff of Prime Minister Yitzhak Rabin, to make sure that the Israeli government actually supported the effort. If they felt it to be counterproductive, of course, we would have refrained. The whole point was to advance the interests of peace, as perceived by Egypt, Jordan, and Israel.

When I presented the plan to the ARZA national board a few months before departure, I expected enthusiastic praise. Nothing like this was ever done before, and overnight, our organization was the talk of the movement. I was crestfallen, therefore, to face vociferous opposition from some trustees. "We are a Zionist organization, and Jordan is still technically at war with Israel," they argued. "We have no business bringing dozens of rabbis to a country that does not recognize Israel."

I was incredulous. First, because I had already committed to the rabbis. More importantly, the objective of the mission was to promote peace. Peace is Judaism's most passionate yearning. Our movement is liberal—we were excited about the recently signed Oslo Accords and were eager to continue to build momentum for coexistence between Israel and her neighbors. The mission was historically important. All the countries wanted us there. The idea that our Zionist board, in the name of Zionism, would overrule the judgment of the prime minister of Israel (and the king of Jordan) was incomprehensible to me. We suspended the board discussion until morning, when I promised to give my full response.

Overnight, I made an emergency call to my contact in the prime minister's office. When I presented my dilemma, he said, "Wait a moment," and put me on hold. After several anxious minutes, he returned to the line, and said to me, "Ammi, you tell your board that I spoke directly with the prime minister. He considers your mission vital to advancing the negotiations with Jordan. He feels so strongly about it, that the day you arrive in Jerusalem, the prime minister will meet your delegation personally, and thank you for the effort." When I conveyed to the board the direct message from Prime Minister Rabin, the opposition melted away. True to his word, Rabin met us within hours of our arrival in Jerusalem and forcefully detailed Israel's efforts to achieve regional peace.

We departed in January. The rabbis came from every corner of North America, men and women, veterans and newly ordained, from big urban congregations and smaller communities. Like the ancient Israelites who took the indirect path through the Sinai wilderness, so we arrived in Jordan after taking the long way around. Since Jordan did not allow travelers to enter from Israel, we traveled to Eilat, the southern tip of Israel, took a bus to Nuweiba, in the Egyptian Sinai desert, and from there embarked upon a ferry to Aqaba, in Jordan, arriving at nightfall. What could be traversed today in a few minutes took us the better part of a day.

The next morning, after spending several hours in Petra, our two busloads of Reform rabbis made their way to Amman. The tension mounted with every passing hour. Intimidating black cars began trailing us. Soon, several of those vehicles also eased in front of the buses. Moments later, a couple of burly mustached men entered each bus and sat in the front seats. These guys were part of the king's security apparatus, there to protect us from multiplying and intensifying death threats. Word had gotten out that we were in Jordan, and we were being watched. Many Jordanians were enraged by our visit.

By the time we rolled into the Intercontinental Hotel in Amman, we were front-page news. It seemed to me that the entire international media stationed in Jordan was waiting for us. What else did they have to do in Amman on a slow news day? I stepped off the bus and was blinded by strobe lights piercing the night. Cameras clicked wildly, and helicopters whirred above us. "Who is the leader of the group?" the reporters and photographers shouted. That was it: my cover was blown! I had a growing sense of dread that those who wanted to do us harm now knew who I was and where to find me. I vividly remember giving an interview to BBC radio in London from my hotel room, jamming a chair under the doorknob to prevent a break-in (as if that would have made any difference). It was an anxious, sleepless night. I lay, wide-eyed, in bed, my imagination running wild. Every creaking sound in the hallway raised my blood pressure.

By daybreak, I couldn't wait to leave. We would be in Israel in a few hours. On the way, we ascended Mount Nebo. In all of Jewish history there had probably never been so many rabbis standing on Mount Nebo! From Gilead to Dan, from the Valley of Jericho to the Negev, from the majestic hills of Judah to the barrenness of the Dead Sea—you could see it all, just as Moses did the day he died. On a clear day, you can even see Jerusalem.

I recited the biblical verses in my mind: *And God showed Moses the entire land that he would not enter.* The foremost biblical commentator, Rashi, understood this passage to mean that Moses looked down upon the entire future of the land. He saw all of Jewish history before him.

And Moses, the servant of God, died through the kiss of God. He was one hundred and twenty years old, but his eyes were undimmed, his vigor unabated.

From the top of the mountain, the Promised Land at my feet, I could sense the cycle of Jewish history—all the trials and tribulations, the triumphs, torments, and the tragedies of our past. For one of the few times in my life, I felt the inexpressible presence of God pulsating inside of me. Ever since, I appreciate better how anxiety and stress can remove barriers that on most days prevent spiritual awakening. The Bible's most compelling spiritual heroes were most receptive to God in adversity. Job, the prophets, the authors of psalms, they all sensed God's presence most vividly at the very moments of their severest distress.

Perhaps it was just the physiological effects of anxiety, but for me, fear-induced sleeplessness primed me to feel at one with Moses on his last day on earth. Standing there amongst eighty colleagues, spiritual leaders, and descendants of a people who should have died a hundred times over, I felt the miracle of Jewish life. After all the centuries, all the tragedies, we were still here, looking down upon the Promised Land from the very spot where Moses breathed his last. The centuries had not dimmed our vision. Our vigor was unabated.

Below us was the sovereign Jewish state. We would be in Jerusalem by afternoon. The Prime Minister of Israel would meet us by sunset.

Bombs and Bombshells

*Eat your bread in gladness, and drink your wine in
joy. Let your clothes always be freshly washed, and
your head never lack ointment. Enjoy happiness with
the one whom you love all the fleeting days of your
life that have been granted to you under the sun.*

(Ecclesiastes 9:7-10)

When leading a delegation to Israel, I depart at least a day earlier than the group. For years, I would step off the plane and immediately start working with dozens of travelers in tow. Inevitably, I would get sick. It happened every time. By traveling a day or two earlier, I have time to recover from the debilitation of a long flight.

It happened that one evening before a synagogue delegation arrived, I was at a restaurant in Tel Aviv with a friend whom I have known since high school and whose wife works in the fashion industry. After dinner, as he drove me back to the hotel, he said that he was on the way to the final night of Tel Aviv Fashion Week. It has become a major event in Israel and a destination for international fashionistas. My friend offered to take me with him, as he had an extra ticket to the catwalk.

I was hesitant. First, I had arrived that morning from New York and was struggling to keep my eyes open. Second, sitting by a fashion show catwalk did not conform with the rabbinic image I was trying to project.

Third, when I am in Israel, I am sensitive to the different assumptions that Israelis have about what rabbis should be doing with their spare time. Most Israeli rabbis don't look like me. They are either Orthodox or ultra-Orthodox and want to be seen engaging only in holy pursuits like Torah study or worship. Since many people know me in Israel, including members of the media, it crossed my mind that paparazzi might recognize me, or that my picture would appear somewhere by accident behind a six-foot manicured mostly-immoderately clad model. I had flashing visions that, somehow, I would be on the front page of a newspaper or in the gossip section, on precisely the day when sixty-five of my closest friends from the synagogue landed at the airport for our religious pilgrimage.

But I was intrigued. Attending a fashion show had never crossed my mind. I set out to convince myself. "How often do I have the opportunity of a seat on the catwalk?" Not fully persuaded, I continued the self-haranguing: "To be optimally effective and helpful to congregants, rabbis need to have a broad range of experiences. We are students of life and should experience what everyone else experiences." That did it. I decided to go. As we rolled into the hotel, I said to my friend, "Take me to the fashion show," carefully explaining to him that it was for the good of my congregants. He smirked in that kind of Israeli way that an American would interpret as "Yeah, right, whatever."

All the beautiful people of Tel Aviv were there—plus me! On that very day, Islamic Jihad had one of its periodic hissy fits and fired sixty rockets into villages and communities around Gaza. Who knows what for, and what difference does it make? They always have their reasons. Before the grand catwalk event, there was a moment of silence in solidarity with the citizens of southern Israel, and then, an outpouring of exquisite beauty, splendor, gorgeous people, and stunning attire.

It struck me that here was a metaphor for modern Israel: beauties and the beasts; bombs and bombshells; yearning to be normal in an abnormal region; a fierce desire to carry on, no matter what. And not simply to carry on, but life in living color: ingenuity, vitality, beauty, the drive to compete with the best in the world and to live unapologetically and unreservedly—proud and free.

Israelis never feel sorry for themselves. They do not lament their fate. They do not despair. They offer the world an astounding example of prevailing over adversity. Look at what a people can do with a sliver of territory and an opportunity for self-determination! Let them shoot; there are people in Israel who will take care of these savages. In the meantime, life goes on. There is more to do, more to accomplish, more to love, more to embrace, more to discover, more to enjoy for all the fleeting days we have been granted under the sun.

Love of life bubbles up from every street corner and from every fashion house in Tel Aviv, from every high-tech hub and every citadel of higher learning. Israelis embrace life with voracious abandon. They love life. They rejoice in life. They reject disillusion and despair. Hamas television regularly threatens

Israelis with eventual defeat because, as they explain, "We love death more than you love life." They are clueless: love of life ultimately prevails.

In the past few years, there is a new trend in Israel. So many Israeli men now cook. It used to be that no one ever thought of the fine art of food preparation. Who had time for that? A generation ago, cooking was not even considered an appropriate pursuit for a macho Middle Eastern man. But today, Israeli men endlessly boast of their culinary skills. When I meet my Israeli friends after long absences, I want to speak about religion, politics, or international relations, and it seems to me that all they want to tell me is how they have perfected the art of baking bread. They think that you have nothing better to hear coming from America than how they have learned to slice avocados in the manner of the most elegant culinary establishments. In fact, many Israeli men now prefer cooking for you than going out to restaurants. It is what passes nowadays for Middle Eastern manliness: a competition for who makes the best brisket.

This is Israel: pulsating energy, ingenuity, and restless talent. The numbers of geniuses nurtured here, the Nobel Prize winners, the brilliant authors, the world-class musicians, the great universities, the amazing scientists and medical centers, the high-tech entrepreneurs who have changed the world: it boggles the mind.

To spend Shabbat in Tel Aviv—to stroll the seaside promenade in the Promised Land, the gentle breezes blowing in from beyond the horizons of Jewish history—is to feel a sense of Jewish ease and contentment that no Jew has experienced for two thousand years.

PEACE

They shall beat their swords into plowshares and spears
into pruning hooks. Nations shall not lift up sword
against nation. They shall never again know war.

(Isaiah 2:4)

To be a Jew is to yearn for peace. "All that is written in the Torah is written for the sake of peace," the Talmud states. Practically every major prayer in our daily liturgy contains an appeal for peace. We are commanded not only to want peace, but to "seek peace and pursue it." Nations need not be in perpetual conflict. If we try hard enough, we can establish, if not love, then at least non-belligerence with our enemies.

Judaism never advocated pacifism. "If one seeks to kill you, rise earlier and kill him," our Sages taught. We are not obligated to sacrifice ourselves to those who seek our demise. Still, while asserting the right to self-defense, tradition emphasized, "Who is a hero? One who turns an enemy into a friend." To kill another human being, even in a morally defensible cause, is to diminish God.

War is horrendous. It constitutes a breakdown of the moral order envisioned for humanity. *You are your brother's keeper.*

Innocent people die in war. There is no avoiding it. The more advanced the technology, and the more powerful the arsenals, the greater the potential for loss of life. It is impossible to fight a war with clinical precision, cutting the cancer out while leaving the body intact. There are no sanitized wars.

The century-plus struggle between Israelis and Palestinians is not a clash between the forces of light and darkness. Both peoples have justice on their side. Both have powerful claims to the land. Neither has anywhere else to go. Both are suffering. Both deserve peace. Most Israelis and Palestinians, like most people everywhere, are more good than bad, more decent than indecent. Most want what most people always want: dignity, opportunity, prosperity, posterity, and peace. Like so many conflicts, this one, too, is tragic. If they could resolve their differences, these two highly talented nations could construct an oasis of progress and prosperity in the Middle East.

The contours of peace are well-known and have been clear since the beginning of the struggle: two states for two peoples achieved through an equitable division of that small plot of earth. Judaism values the sanctity of life over the sanctity of land. Every successful negotiation requires compromise. Compromise is not weakness. Compromise is life. Where there is no compromise, there is suffering and death. Coexistence demands concession.

Making peace is hard because it requires a leap of faith, a willingness to accept the possibility that your enemy can change. Liberals tend to make this assumption more readily than conservatives, who are often more skeptical of the intentions of the other side. I will never forget those heady days after Israelis and Palestinians signed the Oslo Accords. The prospects of peace intoxicated us. It was astonishing to me that practically overnight the barriers had fallen, and we could meet those who, for so long, were sworn to Israel's destruction. Conservatives cautioned that the animosity of decades built up in the Palestinian national psyche would not dissipate quickly, but like any good liberal, I rushed to embrace Palestinian representatives. Within weeks, I organized dialogues between liberal American Jews and Palestinians. I encouraged American Jewish teenagers to meet Palestinian diplomats in New York. I even led a delegation of American Reform rabbis into Gaza, where we met with a group of local activists that included members of Hamas. Back then, it was inconceivable to us that negotiations would fail. We based our assumptions of Palestinians on our assumptions of ourselves. We presumed that they would be as willing and able to overcome the years of animosity, hurt, suffering, and pain as we were.

The past twenty-five years have sobered me. I have come to appreciate better what Jonathan Swift wrote: "You cannot reason a person out of a position [they] did not reason [themselves] into in the first place." In our personal and national lives, emotion often trumps reason. Sometimes, the hurt is too deep, the bitterness too painful to overcome. I still believe that a two-state solution—or some variation that separates these two societies—is the only viable way to resolve the conflict, but I am less willing to ascribe my own motivations to Palestinians. Their history is not ours. Their national and personal experiences are different. It was naïve to assume that the enormous emotional and historical gaps could be bridged, if only the two sides sat down and reasoned it all out. Liberals, more than conservatives, find it difficult to accept that some problems do not have immediate solutions.

I am still traumatized by the savagery unleashed by Yasser Arafat. The inhumanity was incomprehensible to me: bombs exploding on buses, bloodbaths in restaurants, schools, and hospitals. No matter the grievance, how could anyone who cherishes life justify such depravity? I assumed that liberals would be the first to condemn such horrors. It was, therefore, distressing to me that no matter what outrages Palestinian terrorists committed, it was liberals, more than conservatives, who hemmed and hawed, some even justifying terrorism as a legitimate response to whatever crimes they ascribed to Israel. I was flabbergasted that learned students and scholars, trained in the most prestigious Western universities, justified suicide bombings as legitimate resistance.

For a certain type of person who has never experienced anything but Western freedoms, "terror" is just a word, too opaque to be terrifying. Knifing a grandmother in the back is too remote to cut you up emotionally. Such people can apologize for, and even justify, wanton cruelty because they, themselves, have never been knifed on the way to school, never been targets of missiles, never been at the scene of a mass murder, never had to pick up the body parts of a baby. All they know is the beneficent gift of Western liberty they inherited, without having to fight, bleed, and sacrifice for the blessing.

It is not a question of criticizing Israeli policies. No country is immune from criticism, especially on matters of human and civil rights. Jews, ourselves, are our harshest critics. We constantly argue with each other. But the depth of animosity directed at Israel from some progressives takes your breath away. Fundamentally, they oppose not a specific Israeli policy, but Israel's very existence. Adopting the rhetoric and philosophy of identity politics, they consider Israel a colonial implant whose purpose is to subjugate and exploit indigenous communities of color. Thus, they turn on tiny Israel—the one country in the Middle East devoted to democracy and civil rights—with a ferocity that is impervious to reason. Contorting liberal principles, they drain the concepts of "human rights" and "social justice" of their meaning. A bomb that kills ten children is always freedom fighting. An Israeli response is always disproportionate. Preemptive action is always illegitimate.

They speak the language of liberty to undermine the one liberal democracy in the Middle East. They support despots. It is not moral courage but moral preening, a kind of moral pubescence that sees no evil, hears no evil, and speaks no evil of third-world atrocities. It is mass myopic moral malignancy, the rage of the self-righteous. Their "progressivism" is actually a form of fundamentalism—illiberal liberals—as dogmatic, as doctrinaire, and as absolute, as the anti-pluralistic absolutisms true liberals scorn. Under the guise of tolerance, many of them are the most intolerant of people. Dressed in the clothing of liberalism, many have the most illiberal temperament. George Orwell understood the power and seduction of language better than most: "If thought corrupts language, language can also corrupt thought. Political language…is designed to make lies sound truthful…and to give an appearance of solidity to pure wind."

What business do liberals have supporting those who oppress women, gays, minorities, and Christians? What business do free speech advocates have ignoring suppression of free speech? Why are progressives giving aid and comfort to the enemies of progress? What explains the support that Western liberals give to fundamentalist, misogynistic anti-Semites such as Hamas and Hezbollah? By what measure of decency do they abandon liberal Muslims who challenge extremists in their own midst?

Reality is turned upside down and inside out. They pretend that Israel is the worst abuser of human rights in the world. Holding Israel to high standards is welcome. But insisting that Israel abide by standards demanded of no other nation is a form of prejudice. Judge Israel by the same standards you judge yourself.

Would American churches that so publicly divest from Israel convene in Gaza City and spend a year ministering to increasingly oppressed Palestinian Christians? The very idea is preposterous. The only state in the Middle East where Christians are free is the Jewish State. Would student activists and their learned professors be willing to live even one month in Hamas-controlled Gaza advocating for LGBTQ rights, or in Hezbollah-controlled southern Lebanon, or in Iranian-controlled Syria? Lesbians, gays, bisexuals, and transgender people who live in the Muslim and Arab world are persecuted, oppressed, and killed. I met Payam Feili in Tel Aviv, a gay poet who fled Iran and filed for asylum in Israel.

He described to me how the religious police locked him up in a shipping container for six weeks, threatening to kill him.

"For me," said Payam, "Israel is not just another country. It is like a fairy tale."

Where you stand on moral issues often depends on where you sit. If you are an Israeli parent sitting in your living room, awaiting your child's return from school, you are more sensitive to the threat of terrorism than sitting on campus preparing for yet another resolution condemning Israel for all the evils of the world.

Context is not incidental to reality. Context *is* reality.

Oscar Wilde attributed to Thomas Carlyle the idea that you could write an entire biography of Michelangelo without mentioning the artistic works of Michelangelo. Reality is so complex, said Carlyle, that you could write a history of Michelangelo's dreams, a history of his medical conditions, a history of the mistakes he made, the foods he enjoyed, the relationships he had—but never actually mention the sculptures of David and Moses or the ceiling of the Sistine Chapel. Such a biography might be true in every last detail, but the net effect would be to portray a false impression of Michelangelo. There might be 13,000 facts of Michelangelo's life, and you could write many biographies that would never mention that he was a sculptor and a painter.

It is possible to speak about Israel without ever mentioning Israeli democracy, the rule of law, a renowned and respected judiciary that often rules against the most powerful public officials. It is possible to speak about Israel without ever mentioning its respect for human rights, safeguarded by a free and raucous press that is home to more journalists per capita than any other country in the world. It is possible to speak about Israel, never mentioning that there are dozens of human rights organizations headquartered there. It is possible to speak about Israel without ever mentioning that Israel has taken in millions of impoverished immigrants and refugees.

It is possible to speak about Israel without ever mentioning its vibrant and open economy, its great institutions of higher learning, home to a self-critical and politically active intellectual class. It is possible to speak about Israel never mentioning that it has the highest number of scientists and engineers per capita in the world and is a global leader in technology and agriculture.

It is possible to speak about Israel never mentioning that it has signed multiple peace accords with Arab countries and already withdrew from most of the territory of the West Bank. On at least four different occasions, Israel offered the Palestinians reasonable and generous terms for a permanent settlement. President Clinton wrote that he thought the Israelis had made a mistake—that then Prime Minister Ehud Barak offered too much at Camp David.

It is possible to speak about Israel as if the country is a regional giant intent on conquest and expansion, rather than a small state the size of New Jersey surrounded by implacable foes committed to its destruction less than a century after the Holocaust. It is possible to speak about Israel without ever mentioning Hamas, Hezbollah, Iran, and a host of other extremists who threaten Israel every day. It is possible to speak of the West Bank barrier Israel built mostly along the

Green Line, without ever mentioning that it was constructed in the first place because Palestinian terrorists killed hundreds of innocents by simply walking from a West Bank town into an Israeli town, blowing themselves up in a supermarket or restaurant.

It is possible to speak of Zionism's European beginnings and never mention that most Israeli Jews are what we would call today "Jews of color," refugees or descendants of refugees who fled to Israel from oppressive Arab and Muslim regimes with nothing but the clothes on their backs.

Why do the nations rage? You would think that the Muslim world would express some concern, demonstrate some passion, and mobilize some international agency to address the subjugation of millions of Muslims, including the oppression of Muslim women. What should we make of left-wing activists, academics, and intellectuals who accept these outrages with sublime composure and relative indifference, but are apoplectic about democratic Israel's every perceived minor violation? What are democrats doing on the side of autocrats? It is reflective of the mass confusion of our era when we allow a small democracy fighting for its life in the world's worst neighborhood to be savaged by those who claim to value democracy and human rights.

In November 1977, I was an eighteen-year-old tank commander stationed in the Sinai desert when Egyptian President Anwar Sadat announced he would travel to Jerusalem. We couldn't believe it. We thought it was a ruse and went on high alert, fearing an Egyptian surprise attack. It seemed contrary to the natural order of the Middle East that a mere four years after the blood-soaked 1973 Yom Kippur War, the Egyptian president would set foot in Israel. But he did come, and sixteen months later, the Israel-Egypt peace treaty was signed. It has not been a perfect peace. It is more non-belligerence based on narrow national interests than warm interactions of civilian populations. Still, not a single Egyptian or Israeli soldier has died in combat fighting one another in the decades since.

Ordered to evacuate by summer 1979, we emptied the base of everything useful. Egypt would take control of the entire Sinai desert the next day. I remember my last day in Sinai vividly. The wilderness was awesome in its solitude. Just weeks before, the area throbbed to the noise of a modern army on the move. Now, there was nothing left but a few soldiers milling about.

Before boarding the bus, I looked around for the last time. As we crossed the border into Israel, we stopped in front of a makeshift sign that I assume was placed there by a fellow solider. It read in Hebrew: "We have not retreated; we have compromised for the sake of peace." I took a picture of that sign. Whenever I look at it, even decades later, memories of the past flood back to me. It symbolizes what this exercise in Jewish self-determination is all about. It is not about the display of awesome military power—tanks, artillery pieces, guns, and soldiers. It is not about the will to dominate. It is not about might or power. It is about our belief in, and yearning for, peace. It is about the Jewish people's right, like every other nation on earth, to dignity and self-determination.

Palestinians deserve no less. Tragically, peace between Israel and the Palestinian people seems a long way off. But we felt that way the day before Anwar Sadat's announcement, which crashed upon us like lightening on a sunny day. In retrospect, mindsets were changing, but they were subterranean, hidden from view. When Sadat finally announced his strategic decision to make peace, it seemed like it came out of nowhere, but it was in the works for years. We did not notice it because it was happening off the radar.

I pray that Israeli-Palestinian peace will occur in a similar fashion. Until that time, we must continue to seek peace and pursue it—tilling the soil of reconciliation, reaching out in dialogue, extending the hand of friendship wherever and whenever possible. Famed Israeli poet Yehuda Amichai forever captured the spirit of Judaism:

> Don't stop after beating the swords into ploughshares
> Don't stop!
> Go on beating and making musical instruments out of them.
> Whoever wants to make war again
> Will have to turn them into ploughshares first.

Israel and Anti-Semitism

As I see them from the mountaintop, gaze on
them from the heights. There is a people that
dwells alone, not reckoned among the nations.

(Numbers 23:9)

Liberal Jews speak frequently and eloquently about the Jewish mandate of universal repair. We speak less frequently and less eloquently about our obligations to fellow Jews. If you look at the agendas of our conventions, mass gatherings, and public statements, there is no doubt that we are rightly absorbed with the urgency of social justice. But we do not speak enough about our obligations to Jews. We do not emphasize enough the central Jewish principle: "All Jews are responsible one for the other." Jewish identity starts there. The pain of a Belgian Jew is our pain. The fear of an Israeli child terrorized by rockets is our fear. The insecurity of Orthodox Jews attacked repeatedly on the streets of Brooklyn is our insecurity.

Sometimes Jews forget that we are a miniscule percentage of the human race. There are 2 billion Christians, 1.6 billion Muslims, 1 billion Hindus—and 14 million Jews—on a good day. All of the world's Jews could fit into one Shanghai neighborhood. We are a tiny people, about whom much of the world is ambivalent. We lost a third of our people in the mid-twentieth century, and under the most optimistic projections, will not restore the number of Jews who lived on the eve of World War II until the middle of this century—a hundred years after the Holocaust.

We seem to think that we have defeated history. We assume that all those plunders, persecutions, and pogroms are a thing of the past. What folly. There is no past when it comes to anti-Semitism, only eternal vigilance. America, this beautiful, generous, free country, lulled us into a false complacency, impeding us from recognizing hatred of Jews, even when we see it in front of our eyes. Anti-Semitic incidents are surging. As bad as things are in America, they are far worse in Europe. France, Belgium, Germany, Hungary, and Poland are all infected and getting sicker. Parts of the Arab world have been anti-Semitic for centuries.

Jews are not the only hated group. The impulses that lead to the killing of Jews in prayer also lead to the killing of Christians in prayer, and Muslims in prayer. But anti-Semitism is distinctly different. For sure, it is on the spectrum of bigotries of all types, but it is the most dangerous social virus in the history of civilization. It spreads like a plague. It is highly contagious. It will infect every healthy social organism within the contagion zone, weakening society's defenses and devastating the body politic.

Anti-Semitism is a phenomenon of both the right and the left. It has always been that way.

For the anti-Semites of the right, Jews invented Communism. For the anti-Semites of the left, Jews are rapacious capitalists. Both think that for Jews it is all about money and exploitation. Both right wing and left wing anti-Semites are convinced that Jews control the media. Both think that Jews have too much influence over Hollywood, television, and general culture.

Both accuse Jews of disloyalty. Both boycott Jews and Jewish business. Both think that Jews have mystical powers to manipulate society; that there is some kind of international plot to pull the strings of the world for the enrichment of the Jews. From the right it is the charge that there is a Jewish cabal—The Elders of Zion. From the left it is Israel—the Zionist elders—hypnotizing the great powers.

Both right- and left-wing anti-Semites despised us for being a nationless nation, a wandering people with no home. Now they contend that Jewish nationhood is the reason for Jew-hatred. "Jews will not replace us," from the right, parallels "Check your white colonial Zionist privilege" from the left. Both right-wing and left-wing anti-Semites reject Jewish distinctiveness. They always have.

For the anti-Semites of the right, Jews murdered God, or they are descendants of apes and pigs—a parasitical and inferior people, vermin—that threaten the health and hygiene of the world. As T.S. Eliot wrote: "The rats are underneath the piles; the Jew is underneath the lot." Their worst nightmare is that Jews assimilate into the broader culture. Like a virus that overtakes, and ultimately kills, its host, allowing Jews equal access to American life will eventually lead to the demise of American values. Jews will corrupt America and destroy it from the inside. Therefore, Jews must be suppressed, exiled, or barring any other effective solution, exterminated.

For the anti-Semites of the left, assimilation actually is possible. They want it. What they cannot abide is Jews who refuse to abandon their distinctive identity, stubbornly clinging to their antiquated faith, setting themselves apart from the rest of humanity.

Thus, Jews do something that no others do: we manage to unite the extreme right and the extreme left. They are on opposite sides of the political and religious spectrum on practically everything else, but fold into each other at the extremes, overlapping in agreement on their hatred of Jews. One calls it—"Jews will not replace us." The other calls it—"Israel will not replace us."

The anti-Semitism of the extreme right is lethal. These are violent racists who hate many people, not only Jews. They hate African-Americans and Muslim-Americans. They hate Hispanics. They hate immigrants. They hate minorities. They are the ones who burst into Jewish institutions intent on carnage. It is the anti-Semitism of the Pittsburgh attack. It is the anti-Semitism of the Poway attack. It is the anti-Semitism of Charlottesville. It is often deadly in its outcome. It is easier to identify. These haters do not attempt to hide their hatred. To the contrary, they write malignant manifestos of malevolence.

Hateful words lead to hateful deeds. We have known this for thousands of years. The Bible warned *there is life and death in the power of the tongue.* The environment produces, teaches, accelerates, and normalizes anti-Semitism. Hatred, xenophobia, and cultural and racial supremacy do not spare Jews even if it appears initially that Jews are not the primary target. These bigotries are exceedingly dangerous for Jews because they coarsen and polarize American society along racial and ethnic lines. American democracy, pluralism, tolerance, and decency have been good for our people, ensuring and protecting our equal status. Chauvinism and hatred are never good for democracy and never good for Jews. Even if we are not the immediate target of prejudice, an atmosphere of intolerance never bypasses Jews. Threats against mosques eventually lead to threats against synagogues. The moral rot of disparaging the weakest of human beings cannot be isolated and contained. Jews cannot mark the doorposts of our houses so that the angel of death passes over us alone. The creeping shadows of intolerance cannot bypass Jews.

The anti-Semitism of the left is more complicated. If I were to have a purely theoretical conversation, I could accept a form of anti-Zionism that is not anti-Semitic. First, it goes without saying that criticism of Israel is completely legitimate. Some Jews do not always distinguish between criticism of Israel—even if harsh or unfair—and anti-Semitism. Denouncing this or that Israeli policy by anyone, be they Jewish, Palestinian, or other, is not, on its face, anti-Semitic. To the contrary, it is often helpful and motivated by sound principles. No country is beyond reproach. No government is beyond rebuke. All countries do stupid things. They are well-served by friends and allies seeking to restrain them.

Second, some anti-Zionists, Jews among them, sincerely believe that they are opposing not Israel's national existence, but Israel's denial of another nation's existence. They say they do not want to dismantle Israel itself, only its occupation of what they consider Palestinian lands. I understand how in their minds this is far from hating Jews, and how offended they may be by accusations of anti-Semitism.

But, in practice, what does anti-Zionism mean? There are nine million people living in Israel, over 6.5 million of them Jews. What should we do with them? Send them to Europe, as Hamas demands? Millions of Jews would simply pack their bags and leave? Most Israeli Jews are not even of European descent. They are refugees and descendants of refugees from Arab or Muslim countries that persecuted, or discriminated against, them.

In practice, what does anti-Zionism mean? Create a bi-national state? Multi-national arrangements between warring peoples rarely work. Kosovo, Serbia, Albania, and Afghanistan are just a few examples. Even democratic Belgium is at daily risk of splitting apart. Czechoslovakia also ruptured, although the Czechs and Slovaks were the exception to the rule that when separation occurs it is through violence and bloodshed. To say now, many decades after the founding of Israel, that you are opposed to its existence is as ludicrous as saying you are opposed to the existence of America because there were people here before the pioneers settled the land. Or that Texas, Arizona, Colorado, and California are occupied territory, because they were taken from Mexico by force. Or that you are opposed to the existence of Jordan, Iraq, Lebanon, or Syria, because they were created out of whole cloth by the British and the French after World War I.

When Israel's opponents say that are not anti-Jewish, just anti-Zionist, they mean that justice requires dismantling the one and only Jewish state in favor of a twenty-second Arab state. And they say it with such venom. The way they speak about Israel is The Tell that says more about them than it does about Israel. To paraphrase George Orwell, there is something canine in the bark and growl of so many of these anti-Zionists. It is a primal loathing. Hatred of Israel is so overwhelming that it often stumbles into anti-Semitism, even if it did not start there. Anti-Israel activism on the campuses and streets of America and Europe has led to verbal and physical assaults against Jews.

Anything goes when speaking of Israel. Israel is never simply wrong or mistaken. It is genocidal, fascist, ethnic-cleansing, apartheid, Nazi, rogue, colonial: The worst malignancy of the world. The worst! Worse than Saudi Arabia; worse than Syria, Turkey, Russia, China, Iran, Somalia, Afghanistan. "But we have nothing against the Jews," they protest. They will go to lengths to demonstrate that they are not anti-Semitic. They may even raise money to support an attacked synagogue or restore a vandalized Jewish cemetery. Most anti-Semites of the left do not think they are anti-Semitic. They consider themselves freedom fighters, civil rights warriors, humanitarians.

They puff and preen in a narcissistic attempt to showcase their virtue and moral superiority. It is the siren song of virtual freedom fighters—who are always somewhere else when the siren sounds. They hold Israel to standards expected of no one else. There is one uniquely evil and criminal state—Israel. All the rest, no matter their crimes, their illiberal ideology, treatment of their own minorities—their anti-Semitism and racism, their disdain for women and gays, their lack of pluralism, democracy, or freedom—none rise to the level of criminal Israel. Nuance and context are sacrificed on the altar of absolutes, and thus does truth die.

By some kind of bizarre new definition of progressive, a Palestinian terrorist can never be guilty because he is in an oppressed group—a victim with no independent moral agency or capacity. Every Israeli response is disproportional, if not downright evil, because, preposterously, they impute to Israelis and, now, all Jews, the status of white and privileged. Every Israeli action is either immoral on its face or whitewashes, pink-washes, or brainwashes a deeper immorality. Even an attack on an Israeli hospital or a rocket fired at a kindergarten are justified as righteous blows against a racist state.

Some Jews, and groups that have the word "Jewish" in their name, support and give comfort to left-wing hatred of Israel. That phenomenon, too, has been around for a very long time. There have always been Jews and Jewish movements discomforted by Jewish particularism, and who sought acceptance and approval of non-Jews who, likewise, disdained Jewish peoplehood.

In the final analysis, it is for Jews to define Judaism. It is not for others to determine that the good Jews are the anti-Zionist Jews, and that all the rest are, by definition, racists, white, oppressors, privileged, or zealots. What is for others to decide is whether they accept Jews as we see ourselves:

A nation that, sadly, so often dwells alone.

ISRAEL AND AMERICAN JEWS

*God is ever mindful of His covenant, the promise
He gave for a thousand generations, that He made
with Abraham, swore to Isaac, and confirmed in a
decree for Jacob, for Israel, as an eternal covenant.*

(Psalm 105:8-10)

Something is rotten in the state of progressivism that threatens the future of American Judaism. Jews who describe themselves as "liberal" join organizations seeking to boycott, divest, and sanction Israel in disproportional numbers. They lead the attack against Israel with a kind of ferocity normally reserved for the world's worst regimes. Their antipathy for Israel inclines them to join groups that even have anti-Semitic tendencies.

Activists contend that they have distanced from Israel because of the character of the Israeli government and the moral offensiveness of its policies. While Israeli politics, no doubt, plays a role, I think there is a deeper reason for their antipathy. Many left-wing Jewish activists and intellectuals are uncomfortable with Jewish particularism. They assert that it is an anachronistic idea whose time has passed. They sympathize with elements of the non-Jewish left that distrust any form of nationalism. While there was always a healthy tension in Jewish thought between the centrality of Jewish peoplehood and Jewish interactions with, and obligations to, the world at large, it is increasingly difficult for some leftist Jews today to accept that Jewish distinctiveness is a core Jewish value, or even a contemporary social good.

While proponents of these approaches often describe themselves as "liberals," in fact, these attitudes are not liberal. Under what theory of liberalism are we required to discard attachments and loyalties to Jews? Liberals believe in diversity, in a pluralism of communities. We believe in the dignity of human difference. To care about fellow Jews, to feel connected to the Jewish people, and to be attached to the Jewish state are not proof of an outdated, illiberal Judaism. The opposite: to reject these values is evidence of Jewish decline.

Left-wing Jewish activists never seem to speak about Jewish solidarity anymore. They speak profoundly and eloquently about our obligations to the world, bequeathed to us by the Hebrew prophets, but never seem to speak about our obligations to Jews. The irony is that the very concept of prophetic values emerged from those who were fiercely loyal to the Jewish people. At no time did the Hebrew prophets abandon the Jewish particular in favor of the universal. To the contrary, the universal was a function—a product—of the particular. The impetus and urgency of prophetic morality was an outcome of the centrality of the Jewish people, not its negation.

Thus, the very Isaiah who insisted, *The poor and the needy seek water...I will not forsake them*, was the same prophet who insisted, *But you, Israel…whom I have chosen…I have not rejected you, fear not, for I am with you. I have grasped you the hand, I created you and appointed you a covenant people, a light of nations, opening eyes deprived of light.*

The very Micah who declared, *What does God require of you? Only this: to do justice, love mercy and walk humbly with your God,* was the same prophet who declared, *God will take us back in love.*

The very Zechariah who preached, *Execute true justice, deal loyally and compassionately with one another. Do not defraud the widow, the orphan, the stranger and the poor,* was the same prophet who preached, *I have returned to Zion, and I will dwell in Jerusalem.*

The very Malachi who said, *Have we not all one Father? Did not one God create us?* was the same prophet who said, *They shall be My treasured possession.*

Some left-wing Jewish activists contend that alienation from Israel, especially among the younger generations, is a result of the failures of the American Jewish establishment. Rabbis, synagogues, and Jewish defense organizations and federations such as AIPAC (American Israel Public Affairs Committee) bear central responsibility for pushing Jews away from Israel because they have refused to foster—indeed, have actively opposed—a Zionism that challenges Israel's behavior on the West Bank.

These activists have misdiagnosed the problem. Do they honestly believe that if rabbis and other American Jewish leaders only criticized Israel more, American Jews would be less alienated from Israel? That the reason young Jews, especially, are increasingly distanced from Israel is because we are all marching in lockstep with some neo-conservative philosophy that has overtaken American Judaism? Is there a shortage of Jewish organizations that criticize Israel? A friendlier Israeli approach to the concerns and sensitivities of American Jews—both in terms of Israeli policies toward the Palestinians, and in matters related to religious pluralism in Israel—would certainly be helpful. But even if peace were to break out tomorrow between Israel and all its neighbors, American Jews would still be increasingly alienated from Israel.

The reason is that, fundamentally, a strong and positive relationship with Israel does not rest on politics, policies, or organizational outlets. It rests on Jewish commitment. The reason that American Jews are less attached to Israel is that they are less attached to Judaism. Anyone who has spent any time with the grassroots of the American Jewish community knows that identification with Israel tends to be in direct proportion to identification with Judaism. Identification with Israel is the consequence of Jewish identity, not its cause—especially for younger Jews. Jews identify with Israel if they identify with Judaism. If they do not identify with Judaism, they tend not to have strong feelings for Israel. The main reason that Orthodox Jews identify more with Israel is because they identify more with Judaism.

What did we think? That year after year and decade after decade of assimilation, Jewish illiteracy, and ignorance would not eventually take its toll and finally express itself in multiple ways, including alienation from Israel? To suggest that AIPAC or the Jewish establishment caused this alienation, because they do not criticize Israel enough, is foolish. The so-called Jewish Establishment does not create Jews, nor is it responsible for their alienation. The Jewish Establishment simply harnesses already-created Jewish energy and leverages it toward broader goals.

More organizations who more often criticize Israel will not slow these trends. We need more Judaism. We need more investments in Jewish schools, summer camps, and synagogues. We need more Jewish literacy. The primary onus is on us—the American Jewish community—not Israel. We must reverse the mass dilution of Jewish identity. If we do the hard, tedious, time-consuming, and expensive work of Jewish identity formation, then, as in our personal lives, so our communal ties with Israel will overcome the daily crises and tensions inherent in any relationship. Create a stronger Jewish identity, and our relationship with Israel will be just fine. Our identification with the Jewish state will transcend politics and policies because it will not emanate from there. Its source will lie in the much deeper, life-affirming, and eternal wellsprings of Judaism itself.

The painful truth is that American Jews are losing their Jewish soul. We are losing our sense of Jewish peoplehood, and thus, our connection to Israel—the most eloquent expression of Jewish peoplehood in two millennia. The dilution of Jewish identity is the gravest threat to the future of the American Jewish community. For what are the prospects of the continuity of the people if the people are not committed to their own continuity—and do not even agree philosophically that it is a legitimate objective and a social good?

Is it possible to sustain the Jewish people without being committed to the Jewish people? Can Judaism survive without Jews? The will to Jewish distinctiveness ensures Jewish distinctiveness. The will to continue leads to continuity. There is a ferocity to Jewish survival instincts, an indomitable sense of Jewish destiny. When these are lost, the future is lost.

In the modern world, those who are not committed to Jewish survival will not survive as Jews.

IV.

AMERICA

America First

*You shall proclaim liberty throughout
the land for all its inhabitants.*

(Leviticus 25:10)

In retrospect, every impulse of the Trump years was communicated within the first ten minutes of the first speech of the new president. It was the concentrated rhetorical energy of the political Big Bang. On January 20, 2017, assembled before what Donald Trump bizarrely insisted was the largest crowd in the history of inaugural addresses, the President charged:

"From this day forward, a new vision will govern our land. From this day forward, it's going to be only America first, America first…. America will start winning again, winning like never before…. At the bedrock of our politics will be total allegiance to the United States of America, and through our loyalty to our country, we will rediscover our loyalty to each other."

The phrase "America First" has a troubled past. In the years before Pearl Harbor, the most prominent group advocating non-intervention in Europe was the America First Committee. At one point, up to 80 percent of Americans opposed military intervention. But the America First Committee went further, believing that reconciliation with Hitler was possible and desirable. In that sense, the America First Committee was our own appeasement movement. Not only did it oppose military intervention, it opposed military support for Britain, the only democracy still standing. "It is not the duty of the United States to police the world," they said.

Like 21st century America Firsters, those of the last century demanded total allegiance. Whoever had a different position, whoever advocated intervention, by definition, did not place American interests first. If you agreed that we should stay out of the war, you were a loyal patriot. If you disagreed, if you thought that American interests required joining the fight against Nazi Germany, you must have conflicting loyalties. Thus, what began as a legitimate discussion over the wisdom of American intervention quickly dissolved into xenophobia, intolerance, and anti-Semitism. The slogan "America First" became a club to wield accusations of disloyalty.

The best-known spokesman for the America First Committee was Charles Lindbergh. He accused American Jews of leading the rush to war. With eerie similarities to Hitler's 1939 Reichstag speech two years before, foretelling the total destruction of European Jewry, Lindberg said:

> No person of honesty and vision can look on their pro-war policy here today without seeing the dangers… both for us and for them…. They [the Jews] will be among the first to feel its consequences. Tolerance is a virtue that…cannot survive war…. Their greatest danger to this country lies in their large ownership

and influence in our motion pictures, our press, our radio and our government.

Today, as yesterday, "America First" is a cynical slogan. Now, as then, it confuses dissent with disloyalty. Now, as then, it calls for "total allegiance," a phrase straight out of George Orwell. Now, as then, it considers disagreement unpatriotic. Now, as then, it conflates unity with uniformity. Now, as then, it disunites; it creates division. It seeks scapegoats, leading to xenophobia, intolerance, and anti-Semitism. It pits one group of Americans against another. Someone else must be responsible for what the President called "this American carnage"— those who do not place America first. Who might they be? Mexicans, Muslims, immigrants, non-English speakers, Jews, bankers, liberals, the media, academics, the elites, transgender people? Now, as then, America Firsters incline toward isolationist politics, grounded in a pessimistic view of human nature: The citadel is under attack by marauding mobs. We must build barricades, not bridges, walls, not windows.

Do the needs of others concern us at all? Does America have a higher purpose?

Our bipartisan assumption since World War II was that America is the leader of the free world, a burden we have willingly assumed for our own interests as well as humanity, itself. America is an experiment unprecedented in human affairs. We have often fallen short. We still have a long way to go. But our aspirations are noble. From the beginning, we defined our purpose beyond the narrow constraints of tribe and territory. Founded on an idea—freedom—and grounded in institutions that limit the power of government to restrict freedom,

America proclaimed that all human beings are equally entitled to liberty. Liberty defines America, not blood, race, religion, ethnicity, creed, social status, land, or inheritance. Whoever is committed to that idea is our friend. First and foremost, America is a moral statement. Our founders knew this:

> We hold these truths to be self-evident, that all men are created equal, that they are endowed by their Creator with certain unalienable Rights, that among these are Life, Liberty and the pursuit of Happiness.

Our Creator endowed us with the right to be free. Freedom is the will of God, a principle carved into the bell of American liberty: *Proclaim liberty throughout the land!* This is the genius of the American experiment. America is not only a place or a political and economic arrangement. America is an idea rooted in moral claims. Personal liberty and individual rights are as sacred as it gets in our secular form of government. They are also the founding assumptions of religious morality.

And God created man and woman in God's image.

Each of us, created by God and endowed with divine essence, is equally entitled to human rights and dignity. For the first time in recorded history, the birth of our nation set the individual free. It would take decades longer to free all Americans, and we are still far from our full potential. But from the beginning, America insisted that governments are instituted to secure individual rights. Government serves the individual, not the individual the government.

To be an American is to love liberty. It is to spread liberty to the four corners of the Earth. America is a beacon, a torch, the standard-bearer of the highest hopes and noblest aspirations of Mankind: the last best hope on Earth. Abraham Lincoln put it this way:

"It was not the mere…separation of the colonies from the motherland; but that sentiment in the Declaration of Independence which gave liberty, not alone to the people of this country, but, I hope, to all the world, for all future time. It was that which gave promise that in due time the weights would be lifted from the shoulders of all men. This is a sentiment embodied in the Declaration of Independence," said Lincoln. "I would rather be assassinated on this spot than surrender it."

Jews wrote the first chapter of the right of peoples to be free; a right bestowed, not by pharaohs, kings, or rulers, but by God: *Thus says the Lord, the God of the Hebrews: How long will you refuse to humble yourself before Me, Pharaoh? Let My people go!*

Judaism is for freedom, the expansion of human liberties. We despise racism, misogyny, xenophobia, intolerance, and hatred. We are for justice and righteousness. We are for peace. We are for tolerance, acceptance, and love. We are for mercy. The entire body of prophetic values may be reduced to the one insistence that the weak and dispossessed be treated with respect and dignity. We are for racial justice. *Are you not as children of Ethiopians to Me, O children of Israel? Have we not all one Father? Did not one God create us? Why, then do we break faith with one another?*

We yearn for the day when America will be first in every way, and we pledge our efforts and loyalties to these ends:

First in kindness. First in generosity. First in realizing the American Dream: the dream of equality, opportunity, life, liberty, and the pursuit of happiness. First in harnessing the immense natural and human gifts of this country, not for ourselves alone, but in service to all.

America First to protect the dignity and worth of every human being. America First as a force for good. America First to pave the highways and clear the byways holding back human progress. America First to bring light to the dark places of the earth: America First to raise every valley; to lower every hill; to level the rugged ground and to smooth the high ridges preventing human happiness.

America First to unlock the fetters of wickedness and untie the cords of bondage; America First to let the oppressed go free; America First to share our bread with the hungry and take the poor into our home; America First to clothe the naked; America First to banish the menacing hand and evil speech.

When America is first in these ways, our light shall burst through like the dawn, shining in all the dark places of the earth. We shall be like a luscious garden, like a spring whose waters never fail. We shall be called repairer of the breach, restorer of life.

We shall be set astride the heights of the earth: a city on a hill—the eyes of all people upon us—forever and ever.

IMMIGRATION AND THE AMERICAN DREAM

You shall not wrong a stranger or oppress him,
for you were strangers in the land of Egypt.

(Exodus 22:21)

You know the soul of a foreigner, for you
were foreigners in the Land of Egypt.

(Exodus 23:9)

I ndividuals behave differently than groups. Most of us would never dream of seizing a sobbing child from her distraught mother, no matter our views of immigration. If a refugee child showed up on our doorstep, our first instinct would likely be empathy. His desperation would pierce the lining of our sympathetic heart. When we looked into his eyes, our own dread would stare back at us. "This could happen to me because I, too, am human"—this plays a role in how we engage others. We recognize this emotion when we visit hospitals: a mixture of compassion, but also nagging anxiety: "This could happen to me."

Innate human empathy animates our relationships, shaped and honed by the moral code we learned over time. Two thousand years ago, Jewish sages pronounced the foundation of morality. All moral philosophy since is either an explanation or a variation on this theme:

"What is hateful to you, do not do unto others."

An even stronger articulation of the biblical command to love your neighbor as yourself, the Sages asserted that morality is best understood through personal relationships. We are most aware of our moral obligations when we experience moral offense ourselves. "How does it feel to me?" gives rise to an understanding of my obligations to you. If the behavior is hateful to me, it is not right to inflict it on you.

Countries do not act this way. Nations have national interests. The state views misery differently. The collective looks into the eyes of a refugee and sees not what the individual sees. The nation sees security, legality, demography, and economy. Rightly so. No country can long exist if it does not concern itself with collective needs.

Thus, the political imperatives of the collective never fully align with the moral imperatives of the individual. Personal virtue does not easily transfer to national policy. The relationships between groups, domestically, and countries, internationally, are dominated by power and interests. While we may voluntarily compromise our own needs to those of others, collectives generally do not. For example, charity reduces our net worth. We give, nonetheless, because other motivations drive us: compassion, empathy, ideological sympathy, or personal relationships. It is not how countries behave. The American foreign aid budget is not about charity or compassion. It is about national interests.

And yet, our country cannot only be about power, interests, and realpolitik. It must also reflect our highest moral aspirations, what Abraham Lincoln called "the eternal struggle between right and wrong." Human beings cannot survive on power alone. Self-interest is not our only motivation. We need love in our lives. We need friendship, compassion, gentleness. We need meaning. While the state has national interests, and must be powerful to ensure individual happiness, it must also be just. Otherwise, the internal contradictions will overwhelm us, weakening the nation itself. In free societies, moral cohesion is what makes us strong. "Let us have faith," Lincoln urged, "that right makes might, and in that faith, let us, to the end, dare to do our duty as we understand it."

"Right makes might" is the Jewish faith as well. In fact, Lincoln probably learned it from Judaism—he was an avid student of the Bible: *You who turn justice into wormwood and hurl righteousness to the ground.... God shall hurl destruction upon your strongholds so that ruin comes upon your fortresses,* Amos proclaimed.

At the center of the prophetic tradition is a dire warning that society cannot ignore justice and righteousness. It is not all about power, politics, preeminence, and profit. If the collective disregards conscience, sooner or later, the nation, itself, will collapse. We will prey on each other like the beasts of the field. The Torah, the Hebrew prophets, and the rabbinic tradition all assert that the very future of the nation is dependent upon its moral vigor.

Micah warns:

Hear this you rulers of the House of Jacob. You chiefs of the House of Israel who detest justice and make crooked all that is straight; who build Zion with crime and Jerusalem with iniquity. Because of you, Zion shall be plowed as a field, and Jerusalem shall become heaps of ruins.

Religion has an especially important role to play in free societies. We have moral imagination. Love of right conduct is the heart of the religious enterprise. We know how cruel human beings can be. We know how weak we can be—how cowardly—how easily our lifelong convictions can be set aside in one fell swoop of fear and anxiety. We know how selfish, domineering, and rapacious we are—and thus—how dangerous we can be.

When it comes to the question of immigration, it is right and proper for political leaders to consider the nation's economic and strategic interests. This is their job, the reason we hire them.

But religious leaders also have a job. We are not politicians. Our job is to remind the nation of our moral imperatives, and to the end, we must do our duty as we understand it. We are driven, not by what is popular, but by what is right, not by the words of pollsters but by the words of God: *Love the foreigner. Defend the orphan and the widow.* Practitioners of realpolitik assert that words like compassion, empathy, love, sacrifice, fairness, truth, honesty, right, and wrong have nothing to do with policy, foreign or domestic. The only principle relevant to collective action is "interests." It is our job to push back; to insist that individual needs are part of the collective's interests.

We have an obligation by virtue of American exceptionalism to be generous. The American Dream entitles others to be *dreamers*. It is striking, and telling, that so many of the inventors of cutting-edge 21st-century technologies are immigrants. Many of the scientists and industrialists who developed and distributed COVID-19 vaccines were immigrants. We are a country of immigrants. Immigration strengthens America.

Jews have a special obligation to protect the weak. History cast us into the role of perpetual wanderers: the wandering Jews. We are a refugee people. We are, or should be, especially sensitive to the well-off turning their backs on human suffering, unwilling to stare it in the face, or only pretending to care. We know what it feels like to be uprooted. We know what it feels like to be dislocated. We know what it feels like to be exiled, scorned, and hated. We know the loneliness, the sadness, the emptiness that never fully disappears. Most of us ended up here in the first place because not too long ago someone in our family immigrated, most often fleeing persecution, poverty, or oppression. They turned to a country that gathered in, and embraced, the huddled masses yearning to breathe free.

American Jews may be comfortable now, but three generations should not dim our memory or dull our moral sensitivity. We do not have to go all the way back to Egypt. We only have to recall our parents and grandparents. We were the wretched refuse that no one wanted. The world shut its doors to us too. Still living among us are survivors of the great inferno. One remarkable Afghani refugee I met in Salonika, Greece reminded me that the only difference between us is that he was born in Afghanistan and I was not. Most Jews live in America because of a decision of an ancestor who, whether by foresight or fortune, decided to leave before the Gates of Hell bolted shut. Many of our ancestors who disembarked on Ellis Island could not speak English. Had that been a condition of immigration, we would not likely be Americans, or even alive. The accusations directed at immigrants today were the ones directed at us yesterday.

It is hard for human beings to step into another's shoes, particularly with regard to immigrants, refugees, and strangers, millions of people we do not know. We cannot even grasp the magnitude of millions. We are better able to relate to our own suffering. For this reason, the Torah emphasized repeatedly, *Remember that you were oppressed in the Land of Egypt.*

To step into the other's shoes is the beginning of morality and the first step of compassion. To step into the shoes of the persecuted, the weak, and the dispossessed is to step away from cynicism, sarcasm, and scorn. When we step into the shoes of the dispossessed, we see not a Mexican, an African, an Afghani, or an Iranian. We see a child of God.

When Moses approached the burning bush, God instructed him to take off his sandals. Why, asked Jewish sages, did God insist that Moses walk barefoot? They answered that God wanted the rocks on Mount Sinai to cut into Moses's feet so that he would feel the pain of human suffering. When we recognize the suffering of others, when we feel their pain cutting into our own bodies, only then can we assume responsibility for God's suffering creatures.

In 2017, I visited several refugee camps in Greece, during the height of the migration crisis. In one facility, I met the most delightful, vivacious, energetic young girl from Syria. She looked to me about eight years old. I never even asked her name because our hosts who ran the camp discouraged us from interacting with the children. They did not want them to grow attached to adults who would leave them within the hour. But I couldn't help myself. This young girl just saddled up beside me seeking attention, as children have done since the beginning of time. We could not communicate through the spoken word—I did not know Arabic and the child did not know English. Still, to her delight, I gave her some sweets and little trinkets that were in my pocket. She kept on engaging, kept on smiling, kept on laughing for at least ten minutes.

I did not see an undocumented horde threatening to break down the doors of freedom. I did not see a security risk, a threat to the free world. I saw a child who miraculously found her way out of Sheol. I felt her laughter. It penetrated my very being. Even years later, I remember those unique vibrations of pleasure that her laughter produced in me. It was the most pleasing sound in all existence. A child traumatized in Dante's Inferno was laughing!

Is it not the natural order of things for adults to offer mercy and protection to suffering and endangered children?

I do not know what happened to this girl. While many thousands of refugees are still languishing in decrepit holding facilities in Europe, I hope, and assume, that some country took this enchanting child in. What bothers me most is not the good-faith decisions of policymakers who, sincerely weighing the national interest, limit the number of entry permits. Rather, it is the constant callous cacophony of contempt directed toward humanity's most vulnerable, its intention or effect to dehumanize them and desensitize us.

We do not listen enough. If we do not listen, we cannot hear children laughing. The laughter of a child! The happiest sound in all existence.

If we do not listen, we cannot hear children crying. The sobs of desperate children: the saddest sound in all existence.

OUR SACRED HONOR

I will honor those who honor Me. Those who
dishonor Me shall be lightly esteemed.

(I Samuel 2:30)

The moral turbulence of Donald Trump's presidency was rooted in his lowly character. He had a kind of amoral worldview. Whatever served his political interests prevailed, even at the expense of the national interest he swore to preserve, protect, and defend.

We have had dishonorable presidents before. None, however, were as shameless as Donald Trump. Shamelessness made Trump a genius at lying. A person who does not feel shame can get away with much more than the rest of us. He can lie with impunity. Fewer moral qualms restrain him. Lying creates no moral conflict, no inner turmoil. Trump lied about everything, big and small. He even lied about the geographical reach of a hurricane, simply extending its path with a sharpie pen after the forecasts of meteorologists proved right, and his proved wrong. My guess is that Trump came to believe many of the lies he told during his presidency. He convinced himself that the lies he told were true, until he, himself, could not distinguish between truth and falsehood. He probably ended up believing "The Big Lie" that he won the 2020 elections and was denied a second term because of wide-scale fraud.

We tell the truth for two primary reasons: First, it is in our interest to tell the truth. Most people are incapable of lying convincingly. Eventually, they will get caught, and their dishonesty often damages their careers and personal relations. Second, telling the truth is about personal integrity. It goes beyond self-interest. We tell the truth because we believe it to be a matter of honor. "Who is honored?" the Sage Ben Zoma asks. "One who honors all people."

The Declaration of Independence ends with these words: "We mutually pledge to each other our lives, our fortunes, and our sacred honor."

Honor is the last word of American independence. It is a moral, not a legal, term. Honor cannot be legislated.

Rights are about constitutional law. Honor is about our moral constitution. Rights are naturally endowed. Honor is willed. Rights inhere automatically. Honor is bred. Rights are an entitlement irrespective of character. Honor is a choice that reflects character. Rights are about the self. Honor is about others. Rights are protected from without. Honor is produced from within.

A nation of dishonorable men and women will never be free. "Only a virtuous people are capable of freedom," wrote Benjamin Franklin. "As nations become corrupt and vicious, they have more need of masters." There may be nothing unconstitutional in ridiculing others' disabilities, humiliating minorities in public, bald-face lying and dissembling, corrupting and corroding public discourse, but it is dishonorable, and we cannot long sustain the American Dream this way. We have pledged to each other our sacred honor. Dishonorable politics that dismisses and disdains decency is un-American. It is why those words, "Have you no sense of decency sir," uttered by Joseph Welch to Senator McCarthy, were a turning point in American history. Smears, false accusations, guilt by association, rhetorical bullying, physical intimidation, and other forms of dishonorable behavior played out on the national stage are un-American.

The assault on objective truth in this country is a grave threat. The assumption that there are facts that exist outside of you—that you cannot simply make up an alternative reality—undergirds all progress in every field of human endeavor, including science, technology, medicine, philosophy, law, politics, and religion. A blizzard of lies blinds us to the truth, making truth harder, not easier, to discern. While we always assumed that the solution to untruth is truth; that the solution to ignorance is enlightenment; that the solution to bad speech is good speech—what we have discovered is that technology has provided comfort, support, and immense power to ignorance, immorality, and lies.

In her masterpiece *Daniel Deronda*, George Eliot wrote this magnificent passage:

> It is a common sentence that Knowledge is power; but who hath duly considered or set forth the power of Ignorance? Knowledge slowly builds up what Ignorance in an hour pulls down. Knowledge, through patient and frugal centuries, enlarges discovery and makes record of it; Ignorance, wanting its day's dinner,

lights a fire with the record, and gives a flavor to its one roast with the burned souls of many generations. Knowledge, instructing the sense, refining and multiplying needs, transforms itself into skill and makes life various with a new six days' work; comes Ignorance drunk on the seventh, with a firkin of oil and a match and an easy 'Let there not be,' and the many–coloured creation is shriveled up in blackness.

Liberty cannot withstand a surfeit of public lies. Freedom requires a level of public honesty consistent with our ability to trust each other. Hosea knew it already 2,700 years ago:

> *There is no honesty; false promises and dishonesty…are rife. For that, the earth is withered and everything that dwells on it languishes. Everything perishes. My people shall be destroyed.*

If there is no honesty, if lie follows lie, then, as Hosea warned, sooner or later freedom, itself, will collapse. Wave after wave of dishonesty will crash upon the protecting walls of democracy, eventually wearing them down. In the final analysis, trust is what protects civic morals, democratic values, and the rule of law. Destroy these, and you destroy democracy's ability to protect itself from itself.

George Orwell put it best:

> [Organized lying is] integral to totalitarianism. Totalitarianism demands…a disbelief in the very existence of objective truth. The friends of totalitarianism… argue that since absolute truth is not attainable, a

big lie is no worse than a little lie...[but organized lying] weakens the desire for liberty. Any attack on the concept of objective truth threatens in the long run every department of thought.

Orwell was right. It is why what appeared to be an insignificant lie about crowd size at Trump's inauguration, in retrospect, was so consequential. A little lie, repeated throughout Trump's four years in office, mushroomed into an attack on truth itself. Others joined the fray, defending the initial lie. Millions came to believe it. Like ripples in a pond, the rock of deceit cast by Trump expanded exponentially, ensnaring more and more sycophants. Jewish tradition asks, "What is a liar's fate? Even when he speaks the truth, he is not believed." No one seems to believe anyone anymore.

Objective truth is so fundamental to Judaism that Talmudic rabbis described truth as God's seal. "The world stands on three pillars: On justice, on truth and on peace," taught Rabbi Shimon ben Gamliel. Remove the pillar of truth, and the world cannot stand. Justice and peace depend on truth. *Execute the judgment of truth, and peace will be in your gates*, proclaimed the prophet Zechariah. Do not execute the judgment of truth, and there will no peace, because there will be no public trust. Those who purposefully undermine truth, who subscribe to a political theory of "alternative facts," corrode the civic discourse and public trust that cement democratic institutions. Once organized lying is normalized, social solidarity erodes.

How many have laid down their lives on the altar of truth? It is not only a question of protecting my right to say whatever

I want to say. It is also that truth itself is glorious. Think of all those spirited souls whose devotion to facts, to objective truth, no matter where it led them, revolutionized our world: Moses, Socrates, Galileo, Spinoza, Leonardo, Einstein. Think of all the medical and scientific breakthroughs that defied conventional thought. Think of history's freedom fighters who challenged then-accepted social truths—Fredrick Douglass, Nelson Mandela, Martin Luther King.

There is life and death in the power of the tongue. The tongue is like a sharpened arrow. Jewish sages expanded on this thought. Words kill like an arrow because they can kill from a distance. It is as if the Rabbis could foresee the 21st century. Tweets can kill from a distance. Often, we are not even aware that an arrow was fired. *Keep your tongue from evil and your lips from deceitful speech.* Jewish sages were so concerned about lies, vengeful speech, and hateful words that they cautioned, "Malicious speech kills three. It kills the one who speaks it, the one who hears it, and the one spoken about."

It is one thing to point out the mistakes, distortions, or prejudices of members of the media. But to describe them as "enemies of the people," as Trump did regularly, undermines liberty. "Enemies of the people" is a political slogan most often used by history's authoritarians and dictators. Mao, the Khmer Rouge, and the Soviets all employed this language. They learned it from the master orator of the French Revolution as it descended into violent madness. Robespierre said, "The revolutionary government owes to the good citizens all the protection of the nation; it owes nothing to the Enemies of the People but death." Thus, social cohesion was decapitated by the guillotine of extreme rhetoric, that, as Simon Schama wrote, "progressively dehumanized adversaries, recognizing no middle ground between total triumph and utter eclipse."

It is one thing to point out the mistakes, distortions, or prejudices of law-enforcement agencies. But to describe them as conducting a witch hunt undermines the rule of law, the foundation of liberty. Arthur Miller reminisced about his weeks-long research in the libraries of Salem in preparation for writing *The Crucible*:

> To lose oneself day after day in that record of human delusion, was to know a fear not perhaps for one's safety precisely, but of the spectacle of perfectly intelligent people giving themselves over to a rapture of such murderous credulity. It was though the absence of real evidence was itself a release from the burdens of this world.... Evidence, in contrast, is effort; leaping to conclusions is a wonderful pleasure.... There are no passions quite as hot and pleasurable as those of the deluded. Compared to the bliss of delusion...the search for evidence is a deadly bore.[15]

"What constitutes the bulwark of our own liberty and independence?" asked Abraham Lincoln. "It is not our frowning battlements, our bristling sea coasts, the guns of our war steamers, or the strength of our gallant and disciplined army.... All of them may be turned against our liberties, without making us stronger or weaker for the struggle. Our reliance is in the love of liberty which God has planted in our

---

15 Arthur Miller, *The Crucible* (Bloom's Literary Criticism, 2008).

bosoms. Our defense is in the preservation of the spirit which prizes liberty as the heritage of all."

We must not let this spirit weaken in us.

We have been so successful; freedom comes to us so easily nowadays that we assume it to be the natural condition of society. We rarely think about the frailty of freedom: how hard it is to achieve and how quickly it can dissolve. We forget that most human beings who ever walked the face of the earth were not free. Most people today are not free. We assume that we live at the end of history, when all the great ideological battles have been won. It is not so. We must be vigilant. Every generation must struggle anew. This is the lesson of the exodus, the reason we retell and reenact the story year in and year out. Liberty is always fragile. It is always at risk. Nothing is permanent in human affairs. Everything changes.

The struggle to preserve, protect, and defend liberty is constant. It never ends. There is no relaxing. Perpetual vigilance is our lot. Everything human is fragile.

There is a fascinating debate in the Talmud on the nature of leadership. A mere two sentences long, it is, nonetheless, among the more profound disputes of the entire rabbinic tradition. According to one view, "As the leader, so the generation." The opposing view contended, "As the generation, so the leader."

One opinion proposed that the leader determines the character of the generation. That national character flows from the top down. Our civilization will be good or bad, moral or immoral; our policies will be decent or indecent, in consequence of the character of those who lead us. The other opinion proposed the opposite: our leaders reflect us. We get what we deserve. Good leaders reflect a good society, and bad leaders are the products of a society gone wrong.

The Talmud, characteristically, never resolved the issue. It merely stated the two conflicting opinions: As the leader so the generation. As the generation so the leader. We have no resolution. Maybe both statements are true. Perhaps they are not contradictory at all but complementary—two sides of the same coin. Or perhaps the real message the Sages intended to convey is that it is in our power to determine the outcome. We all share in the responsibility. We all share the burdens of the solutions.

The silver lining of the Trump years is that he forced us to acknowledge the nexus between politics and character. Only a virtuous people is capable of freedom. A dishonorable president cannot lead a nation of honorable citizens.

We pledged to each other our sacred honor.

Honor is the last word of American independence.

FOR A MESS OF POTTAGE

Remember that you were slaves in the land of Egypt

(Deuteronomy 15:15)

L iberty is hard. It requires constant and loving cultivation. It can dissolve quickly. It is always fragile. It is always at risk. It took 400 years to free the Hebrew slaves. Even after escaping Egypt, it still took forty years to get to the Promised Land—a journey that should have taken no more than forty days. We tell and retell the exodus story to remember that we were there. Remember the pain, the lacerations of body and soul. Never forget what slavery feels like. Never forget the insult to human dignity inflicted by those who dishonor human dignity.

The Bible describes two types of threats. The first is external. An outside enemy seeks your destruction. Pharaoh looks upon the Israelites and concludes that they have become too powerful. He launches a brutal, genocidal assault against the Hebrews, forgetting, or conveniently ignoring, Joseph, who saved Egypt from starvation.

The second threat to freedom is internal. It is the enemy within. Esau, on his own, sells his birthright. No one threatens him. There is no external compulsion, no force, no brutality. Esau is simply a weak man. Hungry after a failed hunt, he cannot convince himself why his inheritance, culture, and heritage are more important to him than satisfying his immediate cravings, and he barters away his birthright for a mess of lentil stew.

Most empires disintegrate from the inside. Rome ruled the world for 500 years. The Barbarians were only the final indignity. By the time they stormed the gates, Rome was an eaten-out hollowed shell. Not one shot was fired at the Soviet Union. It collapsed on its own. Like rust on an iron bridge, unnoticed until it is too late, the foundations of the Soviet edifice were too weak to bear its future.

I will never forget my meeting with Walter Momper, who was the mayor of West Berlin when the Berlin Wall collapsed. He told me that the day the Wall came down started like any other day. He was in the midst of a television interview, explaining that German reunification would have to wait at least another generation, when his beeper began shaking violently. He needed to get to the Wall urgently. It had just been breached by thousands of East Germans. They demolished the Wall in three days. Its foundations were crumbling for three decades. We just didn't notice.

For most of our history, the gravest threat to America has been internal. No foreign army has invaded the American mainland for two centuries. When united, democracies are as strong as stainless steel. Japan and Germany learned the hard and agonizing way: attack democracies at your peril. But when divided—when polarized and disunited—democracies rust, their foundations collapse, unable to bear the weight of internal discord.

We tend to assume that America is indestructible. It is not true. There were periods in our history when internal division was so strong as to rip the nation apart. Donald Trump unleashed years of abuse against American democracy. Wave after wave of verbal, legal, and institutional assaults crashed against our democratic infrastructure, weakening the barriers protecting us from autocracy. His purpose was to divide Americans for political advantage, to pit one group against the other.

We rarely think about the fragility of freedom. Chip away at the pillars, and slowly, but ineluctably, before you even realize it, you will unleash a tsunami of anger and discontent that will sweep everything away. It will spare no one. You cannot protect yourself by running to the top floor of democracy's citadel. By the time the monster wave retreats, it will have consumed everything in its path.

Even Trump's enablers were unable to protect themselves from the passions of the mob when they stormed the Capitol on January 6, 2021. They came for Vice President Pence, who had debased himself in sycophantic and slavish homage to Trump, but now had insisted on honoring his oath and certifying the results of the election. "Hang Mike Pence!" they cried. The mob that stormed the Capitol threatened everyone, Democrats and Republicans. And even the enablers of the Big Lie that Trump peddled were herded out of the chamber, or barricaded in, like frightened sheep. They unleashed a monster that turned on them.

It was the logical coda to the Trump years. An era born in lies, conspiracy theories, birtherism, incitement, anger, division, polarization, and an underlying energy of violence—a strange attraction to authoritarians and strongmen—ended the same way. The Trump presidency was born in brutishness and ended in brutishness.

They who sow injustice shall reap misfortune. Trump's enablers told, or enabled, big and shameless lies, not the little shadings of truth in which all public figures dabble. Why did they traffic in such outrageous deception? They swore to protect the American way of life. They took an oath. They placed their right hand on the Bible that they told us day and night was sacred to them. They sold their soul, their dignity, their integrity, and our national honor for a mess of pottage—for naked ambition disguised as a calling—to satisfy their craving for power. But the con man will always con you when the time comes. A man who can double-cross his partners, friends, colleagues, and his own family will not hesitate to double-cross his enablers. He has no respect for them. He sees how craven they are when they kiss his ring.

Most of Trump's enablers knew better. Nonetheless, they sold our national honor for a mess of political pottage. They knowingly encouraged or fomented insurrection. They will bear the mark of Cain for the rest of their lives. Trump delivered to them judges they liked and economic policies they sought. But at what cost? There is only so much that even the strongest of democracies can withstand without breaking. They sold our birthright—the American heritage that we entrusted to them—to promote their own personal ambitions.

They knew how dangerous Trump was. They humiliated us. And worse, they set back the cause of freedom for so many worldwide who looked to America as a beacon of liberty.

Trump's enablers could have stood up to the malevolent, malicious, malfeasant narcissist at any time. When some of them finally stood up to him, in the final two weeks of his presidency, the bully retreated. That is what bullies do when confronted with strength and determination. They are weak inside. They puff and preen but send others to fight. They will retreat if you show some backbone. Donald Trump skulked away to the gilded cage of Mar-a-Lago. He could not even bring himself to attend Joe Biden's inauguration.

The most important lesson of the Trump years is that character matters, especially in politicians. We must never succumb to cynicism. Politics is, and must remain, consistent with moral purpose. Every political choice we make is fundamentally a moral choice. Ultimately, politics is about conscience and character. The capacity for self-reflection and the willingness to be restrained by decency are critical qualities for enlightened and effective leadership.

We must vote for those who can inspire us to reach our highest potential, who remind us to consider the good of others. We must vote for those who seek to lift us up, rather than tear us down, who seek to unite rather than divide.

The Porcupines' Solution

And Joseph said to his brothers, come near
to me, and they stepped forward.

(Genesis 45:4)

The American polity needs to find wholeness again. It is not that we seek uniformity. Democracies rest on disagreement, argumentation, and debate. We need a system of competing viewpoints, a marketplace of ideas. But today, millions of people on either side of the political divide consider the other side not merely intellectual opponents but enemies. No country can long survive this kind of disunity and disharmony. "A house divided cannot stand."

Americans must now work hard to restore our basic trust in each other. We do not have to love or even like one another, but we must be willing to live with each other. We must be able to cede power peacefully when the other side wins.

We must find a way to reconcile. We need to step toward each other, to draw nearer one to the other. The Bible hints that until their dying days, Joseph and his brothers never fully reconciled. They did not restore their relationship to what it was before the great betrayal, when Joseph's brothers left him for dead and sold him into slavery. Forgiving and forgetting was beyond the brothers' capacity. Joseph remained wary, distant and aloof, befitting an Egyptian viceroy. He relocated the family to Goshen, but he, himself, did not join them. His brothers, also, never overcame their distrust of Joseph, and until the end, suspected that Joseph would take revenge on them. Something fundamental ruptured in their relationship, and they could not fully repair it.

Still, even though full reconciliation was not possible, the family did manage to overcome pervasive bitterness. They called a truce to the family feud. They never again attacked or betrayed each other. Reconciliation saved the House of Jacob. Conciliation that is short of a full restoration of harmony is still better than unending and unresolved contention. A cold peace is better than a hot war.

Some relationships endure no matter what. They cannot cease to be. As Lincoln urged: Americans "are not enemies, but friends." The bonds of affection remain, even if passion has strained them. The monumental task ahead, for political and civic leaders, as well as grassroots Americans, is to find a way to come near, to step forward for reconciliation.

The philosopher Arthur Schopenhauer composed a parable about porcupines:

> A number of porcupines huddled together for warmth
> on a cold day in winter; but, as they began to prick
> one another with their quills, they were obliged to
> disperse. However, the cold drove them together
> again, when just the same thing happened. At last,
> after many turns of huddling and dispersing, they dis-

covered that they would be best off by remaining at a little distance from one another.

Americans are drawn together, and once in proximity, are often repelled by our disagreements. We need to find the right spot, not too close so as to be pricked all day, but close enough not to be left out in the cold.

CANCEL CULTURE

Everyone on earth had the same language and the same words…God confounded the speech of the whole earth… and scattered them over the face of the whole earth.

(Genesis 11:1, 9)

The biblical Tower of Conformity came crashing down. God scattered the people of Babel, instilling different languages and customs. It is a cautionary tale. God does not want uniformity. God wants a cacophony of voices—babble. God wants diversity.

The assumption that no one person, one group, one political party, one class, one association, one professor, one rabbi has a monopoly on truth is at the center of Judaism. Our sages resisted the temptations of uniformity, insisting upon intellectual pluralism. The Jewish way, taught and retaught for thousands of years, is that we grow, we get smarter, we improve by learning from, and interacting with, those who are different. Jewish tradition celebrates when people debate in good faith when they differ with each other in pursuit of a greater truth.

The Rabbis teach: "Every disagreement that is for the sake of heaven"—in pursuit of understanding—"is destined to endure." Jews do not avoid debate. We actively seek it out.

We do not take offense if you disagree. To the contrary, we are offended if you too-readily agree. There is a remarkable intellectual humility at the heart of Judaism: an acknowledgement that without you, I cannot learn. Without me, you cannot understand. We need each other.

Jews argue over everything. The Jewish interpretative tradition is one long, remarkable 2,000-year record of disagreement after disagreement, controversy after controversy, and dispute after dispute. Our sacred texts explode with conflicting opinions of the same biblical verse. You can hardly open even one page of Talmud without encountering numerous debates over seemingly minor matters. Often, these disputes are unresolved. The Rabbis were content to leave room for future generations to join the fray and try to sort it all out. In this way, the tradition remained fresh and ever capable of addressing changing circumstances. Future generations felt that they had much to add to the tradition and were not merely its passive recipients. Layer upon layer of additional interpretations were added through the centuries.

The Talmud describes one long-running debate between two schools—Hillel and Shammai—lasting for three years. Back and forth they went, hurling arguments and counter-arguments at each other. Finally, a heavenly voice descended to the earth, proclaiming, "These and these are both the words of the living God." Even if only one opinion is eventually accepted as law, both reflect the words of the living God because both sides were sincere, honest, open, tolerant, and intellectually pluralistic.

Jewish tradition eventually resolved most of the hundreds of recorded disputes between Hillel and Shammai in favor of Hillel. The Talmud explains on what basis do we prefer one view over another. The law follows the rulings of the school of Hillel because they were modest. They studied not only their own rulings, but those of Shammai as well. The school of Hillel was so humble that they mentioned the rulings of their opponents before their own. They were eager to contemplate and analyze the other side's opinions. They knew that doing so would strengthen their own ideas.

So, if, in most cases, Hillel's approach prevailed, why even record Shammai's views?

First, as an example: if the greatest of the great sages were open to counter arguments, you, too, should keep an open mind. Do not think that you are always right. Maybe someone else has something to teach you.

Second, Shammai's views were preserved to leave room for future generations to make up their own minds. No solution is good for all times. Every problem lends itself to additional problems that require fresh thinking. If we preserve minority views, future generations will learn from them, and perhaps even accept some of them.

Third, to demonstrate how we can argue with each other and remain united. We can have unity without uniformity. Only the insecure are afraid of challenge. To paraphrase Churchill: a little mouse of disagreement crawls into the room, and even the mightiest potentates are thrown into panic. They are afraid of the workings of the human mind.

Judaism is emphatic. Persuasion, logic, reason, proof, vigorous challenge, openness to debate, evidence, and a willingness to reconsider when new evidence emerges—these are the tools of the intellectual trade, and the prerequisites for social progress and communal decency. Reflexive dismissal of another opinion insults us. "Who is wise?" asked the Rabbinic sage Ben Zoma. "One who learns from all people."

Imagine in our contemporary culture wars that a partisan from one side would concede that the arguments of the other side have merit. You could lose your place in the tribe. Social media might excommunicate you. Your peers might turn on you. If you were in an academic institution, or a newspaper, they might seek to remove you, fire you, or force you to confess transgression—the 21st century version of the Church's inquisition of Galileo. Free inquiry, free expression, the ability to freely research and promote a broad spectrum of opinions are fundamental assumptions of Western liberalism. Medieval authorities persecuted Galileo. The Enlightenment celebrated scientific inquiry, even if it conflicted with religion or angered powerful establishments.

Come, let us reason together, Isaiah urged. Freedom is messy. Healthy societies are full of noise. I remember my visits to the former Soviet Union immediately after the dissolution. There was a strange, eerie quiet on the streets. It was palpable. Suppression is quiet. Freedom is turbulent.

It would be a boring world, and a primitive one, if we all marched in lockstep with each other and agreed with each other all the time. One of the most basic elements of the human condition is difference. People are diverse. For this reason, liberals advocate pluralism. Pluralism cherishes human difference. We assume that freedom and unity can be maintained, and social progress can be advanced, through diversity. Diversity is not a blemish on human progress. To the contrary, it is a social good, the lifeblood of liberty. We should revel in our differences, arguing loudly with each other how best to live. One tall tower of uniformity is unhealthy.

Knee-jerk readiness to censor and cancel leads to authoritarianism. There is only one authority, one politically correct speech, one acceptable language. We know where this leads. We have seen it before. We lived it before, in the horrors of ideologies that were convinced that they and they alone discovered the one solution to all of the world's problems. They are about the search for power more than the search for truth:

> One ring to rule them all, one ring to find them. One ring to bring them all and in the darkness bind them. In the Land of Mordor, where the shadows lie.[16]

All absolutisms are dangerous, whether from the right or the left. They come from the same dark place in the human soul, where the shadows lie. All extremisms are a threat. An extremist mindset ultimately destroys that which it seeks to uphold. "To be ultra is to go beyond," wrote Victor Hugo. "[It] is to attack the scepter in the name of the throne...it is to mistreat the thing you support...it is to find [too] little papistry in the pope, in the king [too] little royalty, and too much light in the night; it is to be dissatisfied with the alba-

---

16 John Ronald Reuel Tolkien, *The Fellowship of the Ring* (Boston: Houghton Mifflin Company, 1988), https://www.google.com/ books/edition/The_Fellowship_of_the_Ring/Y3695-45croC?hl=en.

tross, with snow, with the swan, and the lily for not being white enough; it is to champion things to the point of becoming their enemy, it is to become so pro you become con." There are, of course, limits. Nothing is limitless in human affairs. Only God is without limits. Some views are beyond the pale. I will not dignify anti-Semitism or racial supremacy simply because you assert it. But the increasing tendency in 21st century America to affirm one acceptable answer— one legitimate view—is profoundly illiberal, even if it comes from the left.

The price of liberty is eternal vigilance. Fundamentalisms flourish in both religious and secular settings. Some now argue—with a straight face—that the Enlightenment itself— liberalism itself—science, reason, logic—are constructs imposed on the world by white, European, colonial, patriarchal, and racist societies in order to subjugate others. As Clive James wrote: When scholarship, academia, and language get beyond shouting distance of ordinary speech and ideas—voodoo is all it is.

Intellectual fundamentalists, many of them secular, increasingly populate the great academies of learning. Some are brilliant but arrogant. They think they know everything. They diminish, devalue, or disgrace those with whom they disagree, considering them manifestly and morally malignant, indisputably and incontrovertibly ignorant, or parsimoniously privileged and prejudiced. They cavalierly cancel, using their authority as a cudgel of intimidation and capitulation. They are dangerous. There is coercion in their character, domination in their disposition. They demand obedience on pain of excommunication. There is a troubling temperament in some elements of the contemporary left. They have lost faith in the liberal values of persuasion, consensus, and consent. They believe in breaking things: We must smash—obliterate—the system in order to construct a new society. The existing system is beyond repair.

Like all fundamentalists, they assume that the other side is vapid, filled with unbelievers. They wrap themselves in garments of virtue while presuming that everyone else is morally naked, stripped of values. They clothe themselves in vanity, not virtue, a kind of pubescent self-righteousness. I do not doubt the sincerity, conviction, or sense of duty of parts of the new left. But these are qualities that, when misguided, become odious.

The state of American social and political life today is the result—year after year, decade after decade—of intellectual and political neglect. It did not happen overnight. So many, from both the right and the left, no longer seek truth and understanding. They seek acceptance, a safe place in the tribe, a shelter from the harshness of the world outside. From both the right and the left, we have so devalued science, evidence, logic, facts—we are so intolerant, so dismissive, so eager to cancel the other—that tens of millions of Americans have lost their way. They are unmoored. Even the institutions we depend upon to strengthen and advance liberalism—universities, media, theater, film—have become increasingly illiberal and intolerant.

Hosea warned: *They sow the wind, and they shall reap the whirlwind.* For years, we have sown the seeds of intolerance.

We have allowed the foundations of liberal democracy to crumble. And now, the gathering storm.

We can change America. We can reverse the slow decay.

But we must be willing to fight for what is right. We can do it.

America is capable of miraculous regeneration.

It is not too late. It is never too late for America.

THOUGHTS ON COVID-19

Death has climbed through our windows and
entered our fortresses, to cut off babes from the
streets and young men from the squares.

(Jeremiah 9:20)

We have known epidemics before. The Talmud describes a plague that decimated an entire generation of Torah scholars, 2,400 disciples of Rabbi Akiva. Only five students survived. Were it not for the five, Judaism would have disappeared 2,000 years ago.

We have known sheltering in place before. One of the five surviving students was Rabbi Shimon bar Yochai. He lived in the Land of Israel in the second century, an especially brutal period immediately following the destruction of the Second Temple. When word reached the Roman emperor that Bar Yochai spoke ill of Roman rule, he and his son, Rabbi Elazar, fled for their lives and hid in a cave. They spent twelve years there, studying Torah, praying and immersing in deep thoughts. The Talmud tells us that God miraculously provided for all their sustenance.

Their emergence from extended social isolation teaches us about our own times.

After the emperor's death, Shimon bar Yochai and his son emerged from the cave. They observed farmers planting and plowing their fields. It should have been a relief for the two scholars, but their long isolation changed them. Instead of gratitude that life had returned to normal, they raged at the normalcy of life. "The people are abandoning eternal life for temporal life," they complained. In other words, rather than immerse themselves in God's words, the people were wasting their lives on trivialities like planting crops.

Father and son, alone for so long, forgot that real life required making a living and feeding your family. Those long years of social isolation distorted their values, obscuring a fundamental rabbinic truth: Judaism does not denigrate daily toil. Jews sanctify the secular. Farming, tilling the land, work, and daily chores are filled with spiritual potential.

The state of the world so enraged Shimon bar Yochai and Elazar that everything they looked at immediately burst into flames. Thereupon, a heavenly voice proclaimed:

"Did you come out to destroy my world? Go back to the cave!"

Bar Yochai and his son spent another year in the cave. When they emerged for the second time, twelve months later, Elazar was unchanged. Everything he looked upon was set aflame. But Shimon bar Yochai had been transformed by the additional year. He extinguished every fire his son lit. The Talmud states that wherever Elazar would strike, Shimon would heal.

By the end of the thirteenth year, the physical effects of sheltering in place severely compromised Bar Yochai's health.

He developed a painful skin ailment, perhaps from lack of sunlight. He immersed himself in healing waters. The Talmudic passage ends with Rabbi Shimon saying:

"Since a miracle transpired for me, I will go and repair for others." Since God was kind to me, I will be kind to others.

We have in this one passage two models of how to emerge from a long period of social distancing. Elazar came out distanced. He was selfish, self-absorbed, destructive, unforgiving, unsympathetic, and uninterested in the daily problems of others. He may have resented having to shelter in place. His father spoke ill of the Romans, not him. Bar Yochai, on the other hand, developed an innate compassion for fellow human beings. He finally understood the interconnectedness of all creation: that Torah means nothing if it does not lead to restoration, repair, and relief. Eventually, Shimon bar Yochai voiced some of Judaism's most compassionate sentiments and profound ideas: "Arrogance is akin to idolatry," he taught. "Better that you should throw yourself into a fiery furnace, than shame another publicly."

I write these words while still in the midst of the COVID-19 pandemic. I wonder how will we emerge from the cave, from our extended period of social isolation: Angry, impatient, selfish, self-absorbed, self-centered, and narcissistic? Will we want to set the world aflame, to destroy rather than rebuild, unable to empathize with those who have had it worse? Or will we have used the time to think deeply about what we truly value in life, finding renewed meaning and purpose? Will we try to sanctify the secular? Every moment of our lives is pregnant with spiritual opportunity. Even our most mundane daily tasks can birth a new awakening.

It was not our choice to sit at home month after month. It was forced upon us. Still, given the radical isolation we experienced, will we take advantage of the opportunity for deeper reflection? We have a second chance to clear away the inertia, the moral and emotional rot that has accumulated over time. When we get to the other side, will anything have changed?

Judaism preaches the potential of renewal, second chances. Shimon bar Yochai got it right only the second time, not the first, and only after sheltering in place. His mentor and teacher, Rabbi Akiva, was illiterate until the age of forty. The leading figure of rabbinic Judaism started over later in life, the second time around, once he had time to think deeply about his future.

Reconstructing our broken world will provide opportunities to rebuild in better ways, more productive, more just and fair. Emerging from the darkness of the cave, and stepping into the bright sunshine of a rehabilitating country, may restore our faith in each other. The absence of people for so long may remind us of what we have taken for granted. That the clasp of a hand, the brush of a touch, a penetrating glance, an endearing embrace—the presence of others—these are what make life worth living.

I hope that this pandemic teaches us what Shimon bar Yochai learned during his long period of social isolation. Look how interconnected and interdependent we are! One person, visiting one market, in one city most of us had never heard of before, was infected by one invisible pathogen that ignited a once-in-a century worldwide cataclysm. What affects one eventually affects all. United, we are immensely strong. Divided, our power turns against us. Victor Hugo wrote that humanity is like a rope. Take the rope apart, separate it into the small threads, and you can easily break them one by one. You think, "That's all there was?" But twist them all together and you have something tremendous.

We are social creatures. We are bound to each other. Nothing can replace human contact: computers, social media, online learning, working from home, worshipping in our living rooms, Zoom shivas, Netflix, Google, Amazon, Facebook—none of these can replace human contact. *It is not good for a person to be alone.*

We must resist the habit of being alone in our caves, convincing ourselves that we do not need people, that a virtual community can replace a real community. Social distancing can harden and coarsen us.

We have witnessed both the liberations and limitations of virtual technology. I hope that several years after the end of the pandemic, even the most cutting-edge, forward-thinking for-profit enterprises will eventually cease preaching the gospel of distance. Over time, I hope they will conclude that it is less profitable, that whatever money they might save by employees working from home, will not be worth the loss of creativity and productivity that only physical interactions can produce. We learn by observing others. A doctor learns her craft by observing other doctors. She becomes good at it by doing it with others. So what if you can draft a contract at home? A lawyer learns to practice law through other lawyers. He becomes good at it by doing it with others.

Technology is a tool, not the essence. Vaccines protect our cells, not our souls. They end biological pandemics, not spiritual pandemics; a world unnecessarily violent and cruel, where so many are spiritually adrift, cast aside, alone, and aimlessly bobbing in a sea of suffering and sorrow. To cure these, we need different medicines, ones that science cannot invent. We need a shot of inspiration, an injection of meaning, the sense of transcendence that lies within every human heart—what William James called "the will to believe."

Everyone wants to believe. Everyone needs to believe. In this sense, everyone is a believer. Our knowledge of the natural world is limited. There are mysteries of existence that we will never understand. Not everything can be explained. Human reason cannot solve every problem. In fact, it often distorts. We can reason ourselves into almost anything. Even murder can masquerade as enlightened philosophy or high principle.

It is not human reason alone that propels action. Love, friendship, solidarity, sympathy, mercy, humanity, righteousness, goodness, justice—these are not fundamentally rational concepts. They can be and are rationalized, but they are born in our heart, not our head. These are intuitions—emotions—social constructs placed upon our passionate yearning for transcendence, our will to believe. They are what make us human. We suppress them at our peril. Woe unto him who subjugates his heart to a machine. Woe unto her who prostrates her spirit to an algorithm. Woe unto they who worship at the feet of a false god.

According to Jewish tradition, King David wrote Psalm 57 from inside a cave, fleeing a vengeful Saul. David's days in the cave were not coincidental to his life. They were the prelude to, and the prerequisite for, political greatness and personal fulfillment. Alone, in fear, and on the run, David broke the chains of youthful arrogance and conditioned himself for his unique destiny. At this, the most isolated, fearful, and lonely time of his life, David found the intellectual and emotional resources he never knew he had.

My heart is steadfast, O God, my heart is firm. Awake, O my soul, awake, and I will awaken the dawn.

As I write these words, we are living through the darkest, most isolated, and lonely times any of us could have imagined. May this period be the prelude to, and the prerequisite for, an era of greatness for our country. Judaism urges us to remain steadfast, to keep a firm heart. This pandemic will end. All pandemics end. Tradition urges us to remember that if God was kind to us, we must be kind to others. If we were restored, we must help to restore others.

With awakened souls, we will awaken the dawn of a new age.

THE ROARING RIVER

In the ninth year of Hoshea, the king of Assyria
captured Samaria. He deported the Israelites
to Assyria and settled them in Halah, at the
River Habor, and at the River Gozan...

(II Kings 17:6)

Around the year 928 BCE, the united monarchy of the twelve tribes of Israel dissolved. After a century of union, painstakingly sewn together by the charismatic and legendary King David, and dramatically expanded by his brilliant son, Solomon, who built the First Temple in Jerusalem, the monarchy disbanded after Solomon's death over irreconcilable economic, political, and religious differences. Ten of the twelve tribes formed a union under a new king in the north of Israel. The southern kingdom, comprising the tribes of Judah and Benjamin, continued under the line of David. Although oftentimes rivals, the people of the two kingdoms still had a single national consciousness. Their common language and their shared religious and historical identity lasted for another 200 years. The Hebrew prophets moved freely between, and regularly preached, to both communities.

By around 722 BCE, the Northern Kingdom ceased to exist. The mighty Assyrian empire overwhelmed the small country, killing tens of thousands, and exiling most of the rest. In place of the banished Israelites, the Assyrians resettled people from conquered territories. Thus, some 2,700 years ago, the Northern Kingdom of Israel vanished from the pages of history and from the annals of Jewish civilization. What remained of the people known as the Hebrews were the tiny southern tribes of Judah and Benjamin.

There was nothing unusual in the disappearance of the Northern Kingdom. What happened to it happened to every other nation of antiquity conquered by more powerful foes. They were absorbed into the empire, assimilated, and eventually disappeared. This was the law of the ancient world.

The only exception in the entire history of Western civilization is the Jews. Somehow, the weak southern kingdom of Judah survived successive conquests by the ancient world's most powerful empires for another 800 years, until it, too, succumbed in the year 70 CE to the most powerful empire of them all: the Romans. All of today's Jews are descendants of the southern kingdom of Judah—Yehuda. Thus—we are called Yehudim—Jews—Judahites. The progenies of the tribe of Judah figured out how to keep their national identity alive even after defeat and exile. We accomplished what no other nation did. By all historical accounts, there should be no Jews in the world. The Judahites of the south should have gone the way of the Israelites in the north—disappearing into the mist of lost civilizations, their faded remnants displayed only in musty museums and dusty digs.

The Jewish people are like one global world heritage site. We are the only living national link to the ancient world—a link to be cherished, safeguarded, and preserved by a world so intent on saving indigenous peoples.

The disappearance of the northern tribes gave rise to many mysteries and legends. The fascination grew with each passing century. Many claimed—falsely—that they were the true descendants of the Northern Kingdom. For two millennia, there were Jews who dreamt of finding the tribes and reuniting them with the remnants of the Jewish people.

Jewish tradition referred to them as the Ten Tribes, or more recently, the Ten Lost Tribes. Our sages debated whether they were gone forever or simply lost to us but still carrying on the ancient traditions somewhere in the world. Some, like Rabbi Akiva, thought that the tribes would never return. It wasn't as if they all decided one day to go out for a picnic, forgetting to bring along their GPS navigational system, and couldn't find the way home. They were destroyed, Akiva thought, not lost. They were extinct—as all the other nations of antiquity conquered by invading empires. Rabbi Eliezer, on the other hand, relying on the ancient prophecies of restoration, disagreed, insisting that the northern tribes were exiled, not destroyed. One day, they would reappear.

A fascinating Midrash tried to bridge the differences. The Rabbis teach:

> There were three exiles of the ten tribes. One group was exiled to the Sambatyon River. The second group was exiled beyond the Sambatyon River. The third group was exiled to Rivlata. Those exiled to Rivlata—

identified by the Sages as Antioch in Northern Syria—
were swallowed up. (Yalkut Shimoni on Nach 469:1)

The Midrash spells out three levels of being lost to Judaism:
The first is exile by the banks of the Sambatyon River. The
Sambatyon, which was probably a real river when first identified in rabbinic tradition—perhaps the River Gozan mentioned in the Book of Kings—became known in Jewish lore
as a mythical river specifically associated with the Ten Lost
Tribes. According to legend, the Sambatyon was a raging torrent, full of boulders and stones, thundering with deafening
noises day and night, that could be heard even a day's journey
away. Six days a week, it was entirely impassable. Anyone who
tried to cross would be swept away instantly. But on the seventh day—Shabbat—the Sambatyon rested. It would become
as gentle and tranquil as a placid stream until Shabbat ended,
at which point, it would become an impassable torrent again.

The first group of the Ten Lost Tribes was exiled to the
banks of the Sambatyon River. Six days a week, crossing was
impossible. It would have been easy to cross on Shabbat—but
according to Jewish law, it is impermissible to cross a river on
Shabbat. This group of exiles did not disappear. They were
not utterly swallowed up. They continued to observe Jewish
custom and tradition, especially Shabbat. In fact, it was
Shabbat observance that prevented them from reuniting with
the rest of the Jewish people. The implication of the Midrash
is that one day this group will be found, as foreseen by Isaiah,
Jeremiah, Ezekiel, and other Hebrew prophets.

The second group of the Ten Lost Tribes was exiled beyond
the Sambatyon River. They were not on its banks—they were

much further away. They were far more distanced from Jewish observance, and hence far less likely to reunite with their people. Still, they did not entirely disconnect from Judaism. They could still hear the Sambatyon raging from a distance of a full day's walk. This group of exiles was almost gone—they had no connection with Judaism—except that they could hear the river. They were still within hearing distance of Judaism. Though much harder to find, this group, too, has not completely vanished.

The third group was swallowed up. Those who were exiled to a place that was completely separated from any Jewish observance at all—who were so distanced that they couldn't even hear the roaring river of Judaism—were utterly absorbed into their surroundings. They disappeared entirely from Jewish history. They will never be found, because they are not lost. They are extinct. Gone forever.

What a profound Midrash. These are the three stages of Jewish exile. Assimilation does not happen at all once. It is more like the process of bankruptcy described by Earnest Hemingway: "gradually, then suddenly." The first stage of exile is still maintaining some kind of observance—something Jewish, perhaps a Passover Seder once in a while or lighting a menorah. Maybe some Jewish foods or Jewish music, or Jewish humor—and really getting the jokes. These people might still come back. They are not yet gone forever. They may be lost, but they can still be found.

The second level of exile is losing even these connections but still preserving a tenuous link to the Jewish people. These lapsed Jews do not affiliate with any Jewish institution or perform any Jewish ritual, but they still hear the distant roar of Jewish life. They may have Jewish friends who have some level of observance. Perhaps they have patients or clients who are observant. They may discover an ancestor who escaped the Spanish Inquisition or survived the Holocaust, reawakening long-suppressed family memories and curiosities. There are faint Jewish echoes that keep ringing in their ears throughout their lives—not frequently and not powerfully—but often enough as to remind them of their Jewish ancestry. It is much harder to find them, but they, too, are lost, not extinct. They are not yet swallowed up.

Whenever I meet a person who never knew their parents were Jewish—they may have survived the Holocaust or suppressed their Jewish identity for other reasons—and when I meet even practicing Catholics who tell me they discovered Jewish ancestors from the Spanish Inquisition, my response is always the same: "Welcome home. If you want, come learn about yourself, and rejoin the descendants of the tribe of Judah."

The third level of assimilation is permanent. It is a kind of exile that is so removed from anything Jewish—for so long, for so many generations—that separation from Judaism is permanent.

The common denominator of the three groups of exiles is their separation from the Jewish people. For some, like the Ten Tribes, exile is coerced. Judaism was squeezed out of Soviet Jews by the coercive power of the Soviet Union. Many eventually assimilated and vanished. They are lost forever to the Jewish people. For others, exile is self-imposed. They

make a conscious decision that Judaism is simply not important to them—or more frequently, they just drift away from
our people decade after decade. Three generations later, there
is no return. As Franz Kafka wrote about his own family: "…
it [Judaism] was too little to be handed on to the child; it all
dribbled away while you were passing it on."[17]

I worry about American Jews. I always have, but since the
pandemic struck, my concerns have intensified.

My message to American Jews is this: We are entering the
third year of enforced separation. We hardly see you—and
you hardly see us. We know you are there, and we know that
some of you are working hard to sustain Jewish connections.

It is a marvel to behold. Jews who never studied anything
Jewish, never attended a worship setting in person, never connected with any Jewish institution, now listen to daily Torah
podcasts, spend time online with knowledgeable rabbis and
teachers, or join virtual groups of mourners, seekers, or learn-
ers. These are enormously positive developments. One computer click, and all of Judaism and the entire gamut of Jewish
institutions become instantly accessible to anyone and everyone. Had the pandemic struck fifteen years ago, before social
media and streaming technology, our exile from one another
would have been much more severe.

I worry that the very accessibility of Judaism diminishes
the proximity of Judaism. I worry that we will be unable to sustain strong, vital, and lively Jewish communities. Community
is what kept Judaism alive through the millennia. After all, if

---

17 Franz Kafka's Letter to his Father, https://tayiabr.wordpress.com/
2017/08/24/franz-kafkas-letter-to-his-father/.

you can get everything you want online, at any time and at your own choosing, many Jews, I fear, will ask themselves, why they need the real community at all? So much of our lives nowadays, so much of what we consume and purchase, is online. Friendships are online. Work is online. So why not Judaism?

However, I worry that most Jews will not intensify their Jewish identity during these years, but will instead allow their Jewish muscles to atrophy. Lulled into a false sense that virtual communities can replace real communities—I worry that American Jews will become Browser Jews, accessing Judaism while reclining in sweats, a glass of wine in hand. You don't have to work at being Jewish. You don't have to actually see people in person.

Know that these are Jewishly dangerous times for you and your family. Work hard on your Jewish identity, or it will dribble away. It is not enough to plunk yourselves in front of a screen and watch. To observe a thing is not the thing itself. Do Jewish things.

Recite the Shema with your toddlers before they go to sleep. Observe Shabbat at home. Light the candles with your children. We know that something as simple and as basic as lighting Shabbat candles has a powerful long-term effect on children. We know that home observance is the single greatest influence on the Jewish identity of our kids.

Read Jewish books. Study Torah. Access one of the thousands of classes now online and then discuss it with your family. Let your children see you open a page of the Bible. Why should they see you only reading legal briefs or quarterly profit reports? Why not also the reports of our prophets and sages, the great texts of our people that inspired the great texts of other people?

Most of all: love Judaism. "What we have loved, others will love," wrote Wordsworth, "and we will teach them how."

And then, when the time is right, return to the synagogue. Do not take anything for granted. Not the miracle of Jewish survival, not your Jewish identity, and not the synagogue. Do not take for granted that Judaism will simply appear on your screen, that it will always be there. You must cherish and support Jewish institutions if you want them to survive. Without Jewish institutions, there is no Jewish community. And without Jewish community, there is no Judaism.

We have so much to offer our world.

The small, weak Middle Eastern tribe of Judah drew the map that led to the West. Fundamental concepts of liberty, social responsibility, justice, equality, wisdom, humility—all of these came from that ancient tribe that never vanished.

This is your heritage, handed down to you from the mists of antiquity, and improbably sustained generation after generation until finally placed in your lap. Why in the world would you want to go into exile? And where would you go? There is no more exquisite oasis than what you already have.

Those of you who are packing your bags, or have already reached the banks of the Sambatyon, your exile is not yet permanent. As long as you can still hear the roaring river of Judaism, it is not too late. If you want to be found, we will find you.

Rivers capture a prominent space in Jewish tradition. To reach the Promised Land, the people of Israel had to cross the Jordan River. We read in the Talmud of Rabbi Zera, who went up to the Land of Israel and reached the Jordan, at the very embankment where the Israelites crossed into the Promised Land more than a millennium before. Rather than wait for a ferry to allow him to cross, the rabbi grasped a rope that stretched across the river like a bridge and crossed the river himself.

When he reached the other side, a certain stranger sneered at him: "You Jews, you hasty people, you are always clinging to your hastiness." Rabbi Zera responded: "I stand at the place where Moses and Aaron were forbidden to cross; who can assure me that I should be worthy of crossing into the Promised Land?" (Ketuboth 112a)

Don't wait. It is later than you think. Make haste. Cross the Sambatyon. Return from exile. Rejoin the remnants of Judah. Come home.

V.

GOD HAS SENT YOU

On Human Dignity

I, the Eternal, am your God who brought you out
from the land of the Egyptians...I broke the bars
of your yoke and allowed you to walk upright.

(Leviticus 26:13)

This one verse captures the essence of religion. The imagery is magnificent. You can see it in your mind. The yoke placed on the shoulder of the slave weighs him down. He is slumped, bent over. He cannot stand up straight. Release the bar of his yoke, and you allow him to stand upright. To be upright is to have dignity. This is the central implication. The oppressed are deprived of human dignity. They are like work animals that we yoke to wagons.

We know from even casual observation that a person who is oppressed, a person who is depressed, a person who is beaten down, a person who has lost hope, a person who has lost dignity—looks different physically. She is bent over by the weight of her problems. When you have dignity, when you receive respect from others, your physical appearance changes. You walk upright. You do not appear to carry the weight of the world on your shoulders.

The religious task is to bring dignity to others. We have an obligation to lift people up. A person who is not upright is an affront to God.

There is a Jewish legend that tells of a son walking with his father. The boy is distressed as they pass hungry beggars in the street, people who are desperately ill and those who are enduring great suffering.

"This is terrible," the boy said to his father. "How can God allow this? Why doesn't God send help?"

"God did send help," the father responded. "God has sent you."

COLLECTIVE RESPONSIBILITY

If there is a needy person among you...do not harden
your heart and shut your hand against him. Rather,
you must open your hand and give him whatever he
needs...Give to him readily and have no regrets when
you do so, for in return the Lord your God will bless
you in all your efforts and in all your undertakings.

(Deuteronomy 15:7-8)

There are no laws that compel us to help a struggling person. We are not obligated to give charity. We are not legally bound to feed the hungry or to shelter the homeless. No one will come after us if we spend no time and no money on anything but ourselves. All we are required to do is to pay taxes, a portion of which might go to programs that support the needy. Ralph Waldo Emerson wrote one of the seminal essays of American culture, entitled "Self-Reliance." He captured the essential spirit of this country. Americans believe in self-improvement, self-realization, and personal autonomy. We are rightly proud of our individualism, the freedom to do what we want unencumbered by coercive powers. We strive to be self-reliant.

Our focus on the rights of the individual often causes neglect of collective needs. While there is no constitutional requirement to help another human being, there is a religious imperative to do so. We are responsible one for the other. This is one of religion's central commands. We are not free to walk away from society's problems. The price of freedom is to take care of the homeless, the widow, the orphan, and the stranger; to feed the hungry, lift up the fallen, and heal the sick. We come as close to God on this good earth as possible when we give of ourselves to others. We become ambassadors of the Most High when we reach down low and pull a person up. We find that we can overcome even our own pain and loneliness if we turn our energies outward to relieve the pain and loneliness of others.

In Jewish tradition, we read of a king who asked a great sage: "If your God loves the needy, why doesn't He provide for them Himself?" The Sage responded: "God, who loves both the rich and the poor, wants one human being to help another, and thus to make the world a household of love." That is our true goal: to make the world a household of love. *Behold, how good and how pleasant it is for brothers to dwell together in peace.*

Religion is at its best when it preaches not what separates us, but what binds us together in a common thread of humanity. Our task is to complete the work of Creation. We are at our best when we emphasize hope, not despair: when we acknowledge the brokenness of our world and work toward repair.

We have a tendency in America to magnify our own accomplishments while heaping undeserved scorn on the less fortunate: "I am accomplished; I am in control; I worked for what I have. I earned what I have. I spent over twenty years in school. I have discipline. I have ambition. They—the poor and the unaccomplished—they need to be more like me: get off your duff and start working."

Judaism utterly rejects this approach. First: we are not as in control as we think. Most of us are only precariously balanced in life. We can sustain our equilibrium as long as our lives continue as they are now. But we are one major setback, one employment crisis, one recession, one fraud, one bad decision, one skipped heartbeat, one invisible mutated cell away from a wholly different life. I have seen firsthand what stress, uncertainty, and financial pressure do to us; how they shatter our confidence, destroy our health, and suck joy out of life. I have commiserated with people who entrusted their life savings to Bernie Madoff and whose golden years turned to dust. I consoled people who were laid off or who endured unexpected illness and loss.

Second: Whatever our accomplishments may be, how much of what we have can be credited solely to us? Did any of us awake one morning and say to ourselves, "I will discover fire today. I will invent the wheel today. I will build a computer today. I will devise a new system of government and call it democracy. I will design a capital market today. I will invent antibiotics and anesthesia today"? All of us stand on the shoulders of countless generations who came before us. The whole history of the world has come into our laps. As Emerson wrote: "The human race has gone out before [us], sunk the hills, filled the hollows, and bridged the rivers. Men, nations, poets, artisans…all have worked for [us]."

Only part of our wealth, our possessions, our accomplishments can be attributed to our own efforts. We could not be who we are without others. There were parents who raised us, teachers who taught us, farmers who fed us, police who protected us, political and civic leaders who led us, doctors who healed us, soldiers who fought our wars. Who builds the apartments we live in? Who grows our food? Who brings heat to our door in winter? Who brings water to our showers when we turn on the faucet? Who invents vaccines and medicines that keep us alive?

Prosperity, accomplishment, and success often lead to haughtiness. We are arrogant. There is no basis for a mindset that inflates our accomplishments, as impressive as they may be, at the expense of those who have accomplished less. The better approach is, "There but for the grace of God go I."

The price of individual liberty is collective responsibility.

We are dependent on each other. What affects one affects all. We cannot wall ourselves off from the challenges of the world. We cannot command the climate to cease warming over our land alone.

Rabbi Shimon bar Yochai taught: "[There were once] people on a boat. One took out a drill and began drilling a hole in the boat beneath his seat. The others said to him, 'What are you doing?' He replied, 'Is it any concern of yours? [I am not drilling a hole beneath your seat], but only under mine.' They said to him: 'But you will sink the whole ship and we will all drown.'"

All of humanity is in the same boat. The rising tides threaten all. We are all at risk of going down with the ship.

ARISTEDES DE SOUSA MENDES

And I heard the voice of God asking: "Who
shall I send and who shall go for us?"
Then I said: "Here I am. Send me."

(Isaiah 6:8)

Aristides de Sousa Mendes was the Portuguese consul general in Bordeaux in June 1940. A devout
Catholic, he concluded that he could not remain
silent about the humanitarian catastrophe ravaging Europe.
As the consul general of a neutral country, he could do something that would make a difference by offering visas for safe
passage to Portugal.

Sousa Mendes directly saved at least 30,000 human
beings, 10,000 of whom were Jews—many of them and their
descendants never knowing that they owed their lives to this
sensitive, courageous, benevolent soul. Even today, many have
never heard the name Aristides de Sousa Mendes—because
for decades, the Portuguese government buried his memory.

After the fall of the Maginot Line in the spring of 1940,
hundreds of thousands of refugees streamed south, desperate
to cross the Pyrenees into neutral Spain and Portugal, and
from there, to America, Britain, or any other place that would

keep them out of the Nazis' reach. By May 1940, a mighty torrent of humanity had surged into Bordeaux, which was weeks from being occupied. Men, women, children, the mighty and the meek—Austrian royalty, the Belgian government-in-exile, Polish peasants—they were all desperate for visas. Spain allowed passage through its territory only if one could show a Portuguese transit visa.

On May 17, 1940, Portuguese dictator Antonio Salazar issued a strict order to all his embassies and consulates that "under no circumstances would any visa be granted unless specifically authorized by Lisbon on a case-by-case basis." Effectively, the Portuguese government choked off the only escape route. Day and night, refugees gathered on the steps of the Portuguese consulate, hoping for that magic signature that would unlock the doors of the Gates of Hell. Some could not endure the desperation and committed suicide in front of the Consulate, witnessed by the Consul General.

Sousa Mendes stood at the crossroads. His signature on a piece of paper was the difference between life and death. The stroke of his pen would save, his apathy would condemn. He could do what most of us would do in these circumstances—nothing. He could have reasoned, as most of us would, "It is not my job to determine policy, I simply follow the instructions of my government. I have a family to support. And in any case, what can one person do? This crisis is too big, and I am too small, to make any difference at all." Or Sousa Mendes could defy the Portuguese dictator and obey a higher authority: his conscience, his sense of right and wrong, the commands of the Eternal God. "The only way I can respect my faith as a Christian," he said, "is to act in accordance with the dictates of my conscience."

And so he acted. He knew the price of defiance. It could cost him everything. On June 14, 1940, like so many heroes before him, Sousa Mendes had some kind of emotional breakdown. He lay in bed for three days. We can only imagine his mental agony and spiritual turmoil as thousands desperately gathered each day on the steps of the Consulate. When the storm passed and the clouds of doubt parted, he arose from his bed. It was as if he was newly born, determined to carry out the will of God, come what may. He instructed the Consulate support staff not to disturb him for anything: no food, no phone calls, no business. He would come out when he was ready, he said.

Thus began the most consequential four days of courage, valor, and nobility. In a frenzy of nonstop single-minded heroism, Sousa Mendes created an assembly line of 30,000 visas. Day and night, he stamped the passports of those who had passports; and for those who did not, Sousa Mendes signed transit visas on ordinary slips of paper. He did not restrict himself to Bordeaux. He also supervised the smaller Portuguese consulate in Bayonne, further south. In mid-June, Sousa Mendes set up a visa assembly line there as well. He even traveled to the border town of Hendaye, where he walked the streets, issuing visas on scraps of paper that any refugee presented to him, free of charge.

The Portuguese dictator was incensed. It took a month to shut down the visa operation and to recall Sousa Mendes to Lisbon. By then, tens of thousands had been saved.

Salazar's authoritarian rule lasted for decades, until 1968. He had a thirty-two-year reign. Sousa Mendes was destroyed overnight. Officially shunned, he was declared a "disgraced non-person." The government described him as an emotionally unstable rebel and ordered that no one be in contact with him or his family. Stripped of his right to practice law, his diplomatic status, his pension, he lost everything: his good name, position, standing, income. He lost all his wealth. He lost all his friends. He lost his family, who were blacklisted. His wife, Angelina, died three years after the war. All but one of his fourteen children emigrated from Portugal. Sousa Mendes himself spent his final years disgraced and impoverished, taking meals at a soup kitchen. In 1954, he died penniless in a Franciscan monastery. No one paid any attention. There were no obituaries and no public recognition.

In 1966, Yad Vashem, the world's Holocaust Remembrance Center in Jerusalem, honored Sousa Mendes as a righteous gentile. It was only in 1988 that the Portuguese government finally dismissed all charges, promoted him to the title of "ambassador," and acknowledged the unique heroism of this remarkable man.

Sousa Mendes never regretted what he did. Even during the time of his greatest hardship, shunned and discredited, he said, "I could not have acted otherwise, and therefore accept all that has befallen me."

I can't stop thinking of what he is reported to have told Angelina in June of 1940, upon making his fateful decision that would save the lives of so many, at such a high cost to him. "I have it in my hands now, to save the many thousands of persons who have come from everywhere in Europe in the hope of finding sanctuary in Portugal. They are all human beings, and their status in life, their religion, their color, are altogether immaterial to me." [18]

And he concluded by saying these immortal words, the very sentiments that propelled so many freedom fighters and prophets before him to stand up for humanity and decency, knowing they risked all. Aristides de Sousa Mendes said to Angelina,

"I would rather stand with God against Man, than with Man against God."[19]

18 John Donovan, "Aristides de Sousa Mendes Saved Thousands From Holocaust, But Lost All," howstuffworks.com, https://history. howstuffworks.com/historical-figures/aristides-de-sousa-mendes.htm.

19 John Donovan, "Aristides de Sousa Mendes Saved Thousands From Holocaust, But Lost All," howstuffworks.com, https://history. howstuffworks.com/historical-figures/aristides-de-sousa-mendes.htm.

Olga

Do not stand idly by while your neighbor suffers.

(Leviticus 19:16)

I dedicated this book to a woman I never met. I owe her my life.

Several months before my mother died, she instructed my siblings, who were traveling to Israel to clean out my parents' Jerusalem apartment, not to forget to bring back a certain box. She described precisely where it was and insisted several times: "Don't forget to bring back the box." Living out her last years in Florida, my mother wanted that box in her possession when her time came.

After she died, we opened the box, as she knew we would. It overflowed with seven hundred yellow, yellowed pages of her memoirs. The hidden details of her past finally documented for her children to read. My mother never elaborated on her childhood because, as she wrote, she did not want to traumatize her children. Parts of her life were so painful that she felt that if we knew about these when we were young, it would damage us permanently.

When I learned of the contents of the box, memories from four decades ago flooded back to me. I would return from high school or military service, and she would be at the dining room table writing on her yellow pad. I hadn't given it much thought then, and none at all in the years since.

My mother described her Russian upbringing before, during, and after World War II. She, her three siblings, and her parents, lived in Zlatoust, an industrial city that few outside Russia ever heard of, in the Ural Mountains. Her family was so poor that the six of them lived in a one-room barrack on the outskirts of town. She wrote of the poverty, the depravation, the numbing cold of Russian winters, the gnawing hunger that never dissipated. She described how, during the war, people died of starvation on city streets. She recounted the terror of the Stalin years, how paranoia and brutality crushed the lives of so many of her neighbors.

We never knew our grandfather. We finally learned the details in my mother's memoirs. Like so many millions of others, Stalin's henchmen grabbed him one day, and he disappeared. Decades later, after the fall of the Soviet Union, the archives of that period were opened, and there in the sterile language of NKVD bureaucracy was the proof. He was executed not far from his home, three weeks after he was nabbed, leaving my grandmother alone to keep alive her four little children in a period of world war and mass starvation.

In reading my mother's memoirs, I learned of Olga Gardievskaya. Olga's husband was also murdered by Stalin. Olga, not Jewish, and not related in any way to my mother's family, took pity on my grandmother and her four children. She would bring them food from the cafeteria where she worked. Food was so scarce that sometimes she would steal.

Like a Russian Jean Valjean, she broke the law to bring my mother and her siblings a loaf of bread. She would cash in her own food rations and give them to our family.

My mother writes:

"In those days I was too young to think about it. I took it for granted. But today, I often think what a remarkable woman this was. She risked her wellbeing and her livelihood—she lost her job because of us when she was caught stealing—she risked her freedom, her life, to make sure we did not perish. Why?"

"Now," my mother writes, "as I think about these matters, it pains me greatly. I would like to cry out, to tell Olga that we never forgot her. I am so sad that we never adequately showed what we felt for her. I hope that Olga is still alive. A woman like this deserves to live forever. If she is still alive, I know she, too, thinks of us often. Oh, that our thoughts could meet somewhere, and embrace. She and she alone, more than any other, at great and terrible risk, is the reason we are here to tell the tale. Several times when we were literally on the threshold of death, she single-handedly pulled us through."

My mother writes: "Every time I think of Olga tears come to my eyes. A human being so unique that I am frustrated at not being able to put it into words. I lament my limitations. I would like to write a poem, a masterpiece, to preserve her memory for all generations. To describe her, to honor her, to express the overwhelming feeling of gratitude that we feel for this human being."

"Olga! If I could write, I would write an entire book about her. I would sing praises. I would compose symphonies. I would build statues. I would do all this and more if I only had the ability."

Instructing us from the world to come while we were still teenagers, my mother writes:

"If any of you four kids one day should be blessed in any kind of creative art like music, composition, painting or writing, do your mother a favor. Give prominence to this most unusual woman. I will give you the alphabet. You put together what's in my heart. Not only because she saved us—that too. But because the world is not yet all that bad as long as there are people like Olga."

By dedicating this book to Olga, I am granting my mother her wish. But not only that: I am honoring a personal debt that cannot be repaid. Olga Gardievskaya! The savior of our family. All my life, I had never even heard of her. She saved my mother, and thus, saved me. She saved all the future generations of our family. Dozens of us would have never been born were it not for Olga. Look at the good that one person can do! How the ripples of one righteous deed extend for generations! In this sense, my mother's prayer that Olga live forever has come true. As long as we live, part of her lives in us.

Since learning of Olga, I have thought of her constantly. What did she look like? How did she talk? What was the color of her hair? Where did she live? Had my mother spoken of Olga, we may have tried to track her down. I assume that she spent the rest of her life in Russia, behind the Iron Curtain. If we had found her, we could have helped make her life a little easier.

Had we met, I would have told Olga that we never forgot her. I would have showed her photos of the dozens of relatives who are alive because of her. With the alphabet my mother gave me, and with words strung together from her heart, I would have told Olga of our family's overwhelming gratitude. I would have asked her if she still thought of my mother and her family, and did she ever sense my mother thinking of her? Did their thoughts ever meet somewhere and embrace, as my mother so fervently wished?

I would have asked Olga, "Why? What motivated you to risk everything to save the lives of one ordinary family?" If we could discover the secret of people like Olga, we could eliminate cruelty and increase human happiness.

The final words of George Eliot's masterpiece, *Middlemarch*, are these:

> The growing good of the world is partly dependent on unhistoric acts; and that things are not so ill with you and me as they might have been, is half owing to the number who lived faithfully a hidden life, and rest in unvisited tombs.

We owe our lives to those who lived faithfully and now sleep in the dust. Many of them are unknown to us. They rest in unvisited tombs. But the growing good of the world depends on these people.

The world is not yet all that bad as long as there are people like Olga in it.

On Lesbos

*Give justice to the wretched and the orphan, vindicate
the lowly and the poor, rescue the wretched and the
needy; save them from the hand of the wicked.*

(Psalms 82:3-4)

I stood on the shores of Lesbos, the Greek island fourteen miles from Turkey. Waves of desperate men, women, and children clamored to reach this beach, many drowning in the strait or close to the shore. Many others were rescued, their saviors among the most admirable souls our species can produce: aid workers and first responders who left their comfortable jobs and their comfortable homes, ever ready to wade into the ocean and risk their lives to save the desperate and the drowning.

The other shore, Turkey's shore, is the last cruel leg of a long cruel journey of escape. Those fleeing the Despot of Damascus, the Imams of Iran, ISIS of Iraq, most often made their way to Turkey through harrowing nighttime escapes. They spent whatever resources they had on smugglers. Somehow, they made it to within eyeshot of Greece. So many who journeyed with them were no more; they died along the way. Some never journeyed, their short lives snuffed out by the long reach of murderers.

Lesbos is fourteen miles away! You can see it from Turkey. Lesbos is Europe. Lesbos is freedom. Lesbos is never having to worry about chemical attacks again; never having to face religious persecution. Never having to hear explosions in the morning or a knock on the door at night.

I thought of our own people who stood on slavery's shores: behind them, oppression; before them, the sea. On the horizon was freedom: the last cruel leg of a long cruel journey of escape. Jewish tradition tells us that these refugees massed on the shore in panic. They could not go back. Pharaoh's army would slaughter them. They could not go forward. The ocean was in front of them. Finally, the Rabbis teach, one man, Nachshon, the son of Amminadav, took the first step. Nothing would have happened had not one Israelite taken a leap of faith. Only then, the seas split and the waters parted. Someone had to take the first step.

On the shores of Lesbos, I imagined those refugees taking the first step into the ocean, hoping for a modern-day miracle: that the seas would split and the waters would part. In the Torah, God awaited on the other side. In our times, God's messengers awaited. Good people were there to save them if only the refugees could reach as far as the rescuers could grasp.

Their crossing was unnecessarily perilous. Craven smugglers, who demanded the last pennies of a lifetime of savings from the wretched and forlorn, packed three times as many people onto the rickety boats as they could safely hold. Then they told the panicked masses: "You see that island—that is

Europe—go and sail. You are on your own now." The boats were so flimsy that the smugglers did not even want them back. Either they would hold together for one more fourteen-mile crossing, or they would sink on the way.

Some boats were floating tombs, smugglers knowingly filling only half a tank of fuel, enough to get the boats halfway, seven miles to freedom. "Why waste money on refugees?" they reasoned. "These are the forgotten refuse of the world. If, somehow, they are rescued, fine. If not, who cares, it is not my problem. I was paid. There is an endless stream of desperation behind them."

This is who we are. This is the human condition in the 21st century, unchanged since ancient times.

On one shore of humanity is "the beauty of the world, the paragon of animals...noble in reason, how infinite in faculties, in form and moving how express and admirable; in action how like an angel, in apprehension how like a god."[20] On the other shore, even heaven cannot "peep through the blanket of the dark/ To cry 'Hold, hold!'"[21]

I met a Yazidi young man, so traumatized by his period of captivity in ISIS and his subsequent escape that he could not even be in the same room as he told his story. He wrote it beforehand, and a staff member of the camp read it aloud. In Germany, I met several Yazidi refugees, now resettled. One was a young woman who was a slave of ISIS. What she endured was obvious. She did not have to spell it out. She

---

20 William Shakespeare, *Hamlet*, 2.2.328-331, https://www.folger.edu/hamlet.
21 William Shakespeare, *Macbeth*, 1.5.60-61 https://www.folger.edu/macbeth

wanted to meet, to tell her story. She told it in three-word sentences, her eyes cast downward, exposing agonies that would never vanish.

In Berlin, I met a Yazidi man studying to be a human rights attorney. Upon his escape, he ended up in a refugee camp in Northern Greece with hundreds of other refugees from throughout the Muslim world. Despite all of them being refugees, fleeing the same enemies, the centuries-old conflict between Muslims and Yazidis was so intense and so normalized that the Muslims in the camp attacked the Yazidis in the camp viciously. It is how they were raised in that part of the world: Muslims attack Yazidis—the natural order of things. Greek authorities were compelled to create a new camp, its location secret, just for Yazidis, so they could be protected.

This is who we are. This is the human condition in the 21st century, unchanged since ancient times.

But we are also those who waited on the other side, on freedom's shores. They, too, told harrowing stories of rescue and daring, wading into the ocean to pluck the floundering from the jaws of death. They recounted how they left high-paying, high-flying jobs to attend to the lowest of human beings. Jewish sages asked why did God choose to put the divine presence in the burning thorn bush, that ugly, stout shrub? Why not some majestic oak or pine that would symbolize the majesty of God? The Sages teach: God put the divine presence in the lowest of trees to remind us that God is present in the lowest of human beings. There are people in our world who take that seriously. *You shall love your neighbor as yourself.* Our Sages teach that this is the preeminent command.

Lesbos is the island of passion, linked with the love of one woman for another. The word lesbian is associated with Lesbos. The correlation, first made in the 19th century, was drawn through the ancient Greek poet, Sappho, who lived on the island. She composed stirring love poems, often praising female beauty. Very few of her verses survived, but she must have been venerated throughout the ancient world because the greatest of the great authors of antiquity knew her poems and referred to her verses.

Two thousand six hundred years ago, on Lesbos, the island of love, Sappho wrote these words—fragments that survived to our very day. They reverberate through the ages, reminding us of our eternal purpose:

Come to me, as before,
When you heard my far-off cry
You listened. And you came,
Leaving your father's house.

Come to me now once again and release me
From grueling anxiety.
All that my heart longs for, fulfill.
And be yourself my ally in love's battle.

Some say an army of horsemen,
Some of foot soldiers, some of ships,
Is the fairest thing on the black earth,
But I say it is what one loves.

THE FLIGHT-OR-FIGHT
MORAL REFLEX

But Jonah rose to flee to Tarshish

(Jonah 1:3)

The story of Jonah portrays the human tendency to flee the troubles of the world. Instead of alighting to Nineveh to proclaim moral judgment upon it, which, after all, is the job of a prophet, Jonah escaped to Tarshish, as far from Nineveh as the ancients imagined. The world's iniquities were so overwhelming that it triggered in Jonah the flight—rather than the fight—impulse. Even prophets want to hide.

George Orwell wrote an essay in which he imagined that being inside a whale's belly would be like sheltering in a comfortable and cozy womb. One could keep up an attitude of complete indifference there. It could be the best place to hide from the world's problems. A storm that would sink all the battleships in the world would hardly reach you as an echo. Short of being dead, being in the belly of the whale is the final, unsurpassable stage of irresponsibility, wrote Orwell.

The essential Jonah act is allowing yourself to be swallowed—passive acceptance of whatever happens in the world. Like Geppetto inside Monstro's belly, you can imagine Jonah setting up a rocking chair and a candle inside the living room of the whale's belly. He could read Greek poetry, or study Socrates, a possible contemporary of the author of the book of Jonah. He could be completely oblivious to the outside world. Nothing would reach him through vast oceans of water and multiple layers of blubber. No sound, no disturbance, no disruption. Even the mightiest shofar blast of moral urgency would go unheard inside the whale. This prophet whom God so challenged could devote himself solely to himself—his cocoon of contentment impregnable to the world's cacophony of contention.

To fight for justice is to invite despair: *Take my life, God, it is better for me to die than to live,* Jonah pleaded. He was not the only prophet who prayed for death. *I cannot carry this people by myself, it is too much for me,* cried Moses. *Kill me, I beg of you, and let me see no more of my wretchedness.*

Cursed the day that I was born, Jeremiah lamented. *Cursed be the one who brought my father the news and said 'a boy is born to you.' Why did I ever issue from the womb—to see misery and woe?*

There is so much misery and woe in the world that even history's greatest heroes had moments of despondency. But to disengage from the fight is to leave the field to the armies of infamy and the captains of chaos, who may be passionate, but are passionate for the wrong things. To withdraw leads to a world that Yeats described: "Things fall apart; the centre cannot hold…. The best lack all conviction, while the worst / Are full of passionate intensity."[22] Sooner or later, we will discover what Jonah discovered, and what every society since has learned and relearned: We cannot hide. We cannot shut out the problems of the world.

Our 20th century prophet, Martin Luther King, Jr., said it best:

"Injustice anywhere is a threat to justice everywhere…. Whatever affects one directly, affects all indirectly. I cannot be what I ought to be until you are what you ought to be, and you can never be what you ought to be until I am what I ought to be." "This is the inter-related structure of reality," said King, who offered that much better definition of intersectionality than what faux prophets offer today. King, too, suffered bouts of despondency. There were days when he was so depressed that he could not get out of bed.

To run to Tarshish is to distance ourselves from ourselves. To live inside an envelope of indifference is to live outside the human experience. It is the opposite of safety. To shut the world out is to invite moral chaos that will eventually lead back to us anyway. Human emotions, human unreason, the human vices of envy, revenge, and conquest will hunt you down even in your carefully constructed cocoon. They will find you, even inside the whale at the bottom of the ocean. To be human is to be vulnerable. By empathizing with the struggles of others, we strengthen ourselves. We build immunity to moral disease.

---

22 William Butler Yeats, "The Second Coming," 1989, https://www.poetryfoundation.org/poems/43290/the-second-coming.

As Herman Melville put in the mouth of Captain Ahab:

Death to [the whale].... God hunt us all, if we do not hunt Moby Dick to his death!.... I'll chase him round Good Hope, and round the Horn, and round the Norway Maelstrom, and round perdition's flames before I give him up.... Towards thee I roll...to the last I grapple with thee; from hell's heart I stab at thee; for hate's sake I spit my last breath at thee.

There is no escaping the sordidness of those Melville described as "morally enfeebled," who carry the hot fires of "all the general rage and hate felt by [the human] race from Adam down." They will find you even in the most remote parts of the world. Passivity led to the worldwide COVID-19 pandemic. No place on Earth was safe. Aggressive intervention could have prevented, or at least, diminished, its lethality.

So if the flight reflex to injustice is unacceptable and unworkable, there is only one option available to us: to fight back. The fight is what counts. The fight for justice, itself, gives meaning. We cannot retreat from the world. We are forbidden to disengage. We fight until the last gasp. To fight for others is to fight against alienation and despair. To withdraw, to run to Tarshish, is to allow the instincts of empathy to deteriorate, and the muscles of responsibility to atrophy. We are commanded to act because our resolve weakens when we do not act. There is not enough oxygen inside the whale to keep the candle of conscience burning. It must be kindled constantly, conscientiously, and continuously.

Judaism is one giant proclamation of dissatisfaction that the world is not what it could be, and one giant struggle to create a world that ought to be. A believing Jew is a disquieted Jew. Our purpose is not serenity, but solidity and solidarity. Jews do not regard this world merely as a gateway to the eternal world. There is, of course, speculation in Judaism about the world to come. But our primary focus was always the here and now. For Jews, engagement is required. Piety is in performance. Apathy, lethargy, and complacency hollow out our human essence, the capacity to care about, and empathize with, fellow human beings. Moral awareness gives substance to our limited days, sustenance to our struggle for meaning, and subsistence to our fragile community.

When conscience dies, we die a spiritual death.

POLITICS AND RELIGION

Wash yourselves, make yourself clean. Put away your evil
doings. Cease to do evil. Learn to do good. Seek justice.
Relieve the oppressed. Plead for the disadvantaged.

(Isaiah 1: 16-17)

I preach politics from my pulpit. The alternative would be
a colossal waste. Why even have a pulpit if you do not
intend to influence personal and collective behavior?

Of course, to address society's toughest and most conten-
tious debates is often controversial. So, what? A public figure who shies away from controversy is likely in the wrong
line of work. Our vocation is not to avoid controversy, but to
advance individual and collective morality.

Increasingly, I meet rabbis who tell me that they no longer
speak about Israel in their synagogues. "Israel has become too
controversial," they say. "Too many people get angry with me.
Israel has become political, and the board doesn't want me to
preach politics from the pulpit." It reminds me of the story
of the rabbi who suffered a mild heart attack, and when the
president of the congregation visited him at the hospital, he
sat down next to the rabbi, grasped his hand in sympathy, and

said, "I have good news, Rabbi; the board just voted 12:8 to wish you a speedy recovery."

Our role is not to be so uncontroversial, so bland, as to receive a unanimous vote of approval for every action or initiative we propose. To paraphrase Rabbi Israel Salanter, the founder of the Mussar movement (in the language of his era before female rabbis): "A rabbi whose community does not disagree with him is no rabbi. A rabbi who fears his community is no man." Rabbis do not determine what is right or wrong by polling public opinion. We do not seek to mirror consensus, but to mold consensus.

Our concern is the morality of polices. Synagogues are not political organizations. We do not endorse parties or candidates. Clergy are not politicians. Our calling brings us into contact with the political world, but not as partisans. We are moral agents, seeking the welfare of the nation. Since politics is how free societies determine policies, synagogues cannot avoid the political process. We would lose integrity. We would be unable to look ourselves in the eye. What kind of religion could maintain credibility lamenting the sufferings of the persecuted but not caring about the policies that lead to suffering or the measures that can alleviate suffering? What kind of religion offers beds to the homeless but is unconcerned about the policies that cause or exacerbate homelessness?

Social apathy is not an option for Jews. Judaism is an activist, involved religion. Pursue justice. Relieve oppression. Plead for the poor. There is no such thing in Judaism as abstract theology disconnected from the real lives of real people. We do not speak exclusively of God in Heaven. We bring Heaven to earth through social repair. We speculate about the hereafter, but the here and now are our primary concerns. We do not escape the secular world. We sanctify the secular. Judaism is a religion of potency and protest. Jews are obligated—we do not have a choice—to speak about, and act upon, the moral challenges of our times. Our tradition demands: What have you done today to alleviate suffering and ensure fairness? Judaism insists on liberty, dignity, generosity, charity, and empathy for all of God's creatures.

This is our calling, what we mean by the prophetic voice. Prophets spoke truth to power. Their truth was that collective morality was the linchpin of national security. Weapons of war would be useless in protecting the nation if social immoralities were rampant. Over time, festering injustice would destabilize the country, diluting social cohesion and degrading national unity. Prophets did not predict the future. They were not soothsayers. They cautioned that without changing our ways, the future would unfold in catastrophic ways.

In forty days, Nineveh will be destroyed, Jonah proclaims. Nineveh repented and was not destroyed. It saddened Jonah that the prophecy did not materialize. He considered himself a failure. But he misunderstood the prophetic role. It was not to predict the destruction of Nineveh. It was to warn that the survival of Nineveh depended on its moral character. The salvation of Nineveh was Jonah's highest achievement, not his lowest failure. His story teaches that our efforts make a difference. We can challenge amoral authority with the authority of a moral challenge.

Jews cannot be silent in the face of injustice: "Whoever can prevent his household from doing wrong and does not, is punished for the wrongs of his household," teach our sages. "Whoever can prevent his neighbors from doing wrong and does not, is punished for the wrongs of his neighbors. Whoever can prevent the world from doing wrong and does not, is punished for the wrongs of the world."

Everything we receive from Jewish tradition pleads with us: Get more involved. Be more active. The sages teach that we are not obligated to complete the work, but neither are we free to desist. Trying is what Judaism expects. We know that the wolf will not lie down with the lamb today, nor will the leopard lie down with the kid tomorrow. But we also know that human beings ought to be peaceful: that each of us ought to be able to lay under vine and fig tree unafraid. Over time, what ought to be often becomes what is. If enough people accept a standard of behavior, that behavior will become the accepted standard. Judaism demands that we keep trying to bring about that day, handing the torch to our children when our energy is spent and our work is done, as we received the torch from our parents.

All who call for Church and Synagogue to "stay out of politics"—by which they mean never speak about policy measures that could ameliorate the social challenges of our times, never mention the pain of this world, only the bliss of the next world—condemn themselves to irrelevancy, and even worse, they render religion itself impotent. The assertion that religious institutions should stay out of politics is itself a political stance. It takes you off the field, the public arena, where the contest of values is determined, and leaves the field open to others, opponents who have different values.

In over thirty years on the pulpit, I have never met a single person who criticized me for being "too political" if they agreed with my views. For them, I was a man of principle. Only those who disagreed with me on a policy matter said, "Just stick to religion, Rabbi."

"My idea of an agreeable person is a person who agrees with me," Benjamin Disraeli said.

How true.

VI.

THE ART OF LIVING

THE ART OF LIVING

Wise advice is as valuable as a gold earring.

(Proverbs 25:12)

The Mauritshuis Museum in The Hague houses one of the world's most famous paintings: Vermeer's *Girl with a Pearl Earring*. The masterwork is well known: a beautiful young woman wearing a blue turban, positioned in such a way as to place a large pearl earring as the focal point of the entire painting. As the museum emphasizes in its promotional literature, it is the most famous earring in the art world.

While listening to the headphone recording that the museum provides, I was especially struck by the description of how Vermeer painted the earring. It took two brushstrokes. Two brushstrokes produced one of the most endearing and enduring images of art history. The most famous earring in the art world was the result of two quick movements!

So I thought to myself: Can't anyone do that? One stroke this way and one stroke that way—I can do it too. After I came to my senses, I reached two conclusions:

First: people who are good at what they do make it look easy. It does not mean that everyone can do it, only that some people are so good at their vocation that it seems to lay observers that anyone can do it. It may look easy, but very few people can hit tennis balls as champions do, play piano as musicians do, or fix a boiler as mechanics do.

There is a story of the boilermaker who was hired to fix a huge steamship boiler system. He went down to the boiler room, listened to the thumps and hisses for a moment, immediately took out a small hammer, and tapped a bright red valve once. It took less than a minute and the system was fixed. When the steamship owner received the bill for a thousand dollars he complained to the boilermaker that the whole thing took less than a minute—and so he requested an itemized bill. He received this itemization: For tapping with hammer: one dollar. For knowing where to tap: $999.00.

People who excel make it look easy, but it is because they know where to tap. In reality, to be good at something takes enormous work and dedication. Even people with immense innate talent cannot rest on their genius. Those two strokes that produced the girl's pearl earring took a lifetime of study, practice, and reflection. Tens of thousands of hours devoted to the art of painting.

There is an art to living. It is not as easy as it looks. If we are to be good at life, we must study how to live. Judaism trains people in the art of life. It might look easy, but it is not. It might seem like everyone can do it, but they cannot. You might imagine that it takes just two strokes, but you must spend a lifetime knowing how to paint those strokes. You must work at it; you must think about it, and you must practice day after day, year after year. You must develop enough knowledge and understanding to know, not only how to tap, but where to tap.

Second: sometimes in life, the most beautiful things are the simplest. The most complex ideas contain the purest principles: just two strokes. The most meaningful elements of life are the most basic. Family, friends, community, love, health, dignity, compassion, peace.

No philosopher, no genius in the future, will improve on the simplicity of these elements.

REFLECTING ON THE
PASSAGE OF TIME

We are sojourners with You, mere transients, like our
fathers. Our days on earth are like a shadow...

(I Chronicles 29:15)

One summer, thirty years after graduating from the London School of Economics, I was wandering around the British capital, reminiscing about my three years in law school. I had not visited in decades. By force of long-repressed habit, I found myself on Houghton Street and entered the main building of the LSE campus. Torrential memories flooded back to me.

These were among the best days of my life. I walked to the end of the corridor, entered the last room on the right, and the vividness of the lecture hall astonished me. I studied contracts, tort, criminal law, and jurisprudence here, with one hundred classmates. I remembered precisely where I sat. I pictured where my wife-to-be sat, two rows behind me and a bit to my right. I recalled our professors, among the world's leading experts, many of whom were no longer alive, and most of the rest long retired.

The first thing I noticed is that the beloved creaky history-filled building is no longer called "The Main Building." It is now called "The Old Building." In the past thirty years, the campus has expanded. The buildings that were added are called "The New Buildings." So, of course, that set me off on another bout of melancholia: If I studied in what was then called "The Main Building" but is now called "The Old Building," does that mean that anyone who studied in the Old Building is old? I was still in my fifties. Was I no longer sitting in the main building of society?

I stared at the students. Why did they fascinate me? Did they remind me of me? Was I subconsciously seeking to reverse the passage of time? What I wouldn't give to relinquish the accumulated burdens of three adult decades and relive those carefree years of my student days. Today's LSE students looked like how I remember myself. They meandered about on the steps and in the sandwich shop at the entrance to the Old Building. The café on the street was still in business, looking no different than it did when I would grab a snack there between classes.

Unlike my classmates, every one of the students I saw was connected to a device. They had wires in their ears, computers in their hands, music in their pockets. We had none of these. We had to visit special rooms, called "libraries," to do research. Today's students have all the material, all their books and scholarly papers, in the palm of their hands. They don't really use libraries anymore, at least not as we did. Why go to the library if you can download anything you need? Back in my day, the sign of a serious student was books strewn all over the dorm room. Today, students view piles of books in your room as just a messy room.

Since we live our lives day by day, we do not appreciate the rapid pace of change. But place our lives in the context of a thirty-year horizon, and the transformations are astonishing. It is not only technology. Today's teenagers never lived in a world menaced by the Soviet Union. When I speak with young people, they look at me perplexed and baffled when I even use the word "communism." Teenagers never lived through Vietnam or the Civil Rights Struggle, let alone World War II and the new world order that was established in its wake. When I sat on the steps of the LSE in the early 1980s, none of us imagined that within several years we would be traveling through European countries without showing a passport, or even knowing when we crossed a border.

Time is like a mighty river, a relentless torrent that, like the Mississippi, just keeps rolling along. It sweeps us up, carries us a tiny distance further down the bank, and deposits us on its shores. As Shakespeare put it:

> Like as the waves make towards the pebbl'd shore
> So do our minutes hasten to their end;
> Each changing place with that which goes before,
> In sequent toil all forwards do contend.[23]

The ancients had a better appreciation of time than we do. The psalmist wrote: *Before the mountains were born, You formed the earth and all the universe. A thousand years are but*

---

23 William Shakespeare, "Sonnet 60,"
https://www.poetryfoundation.org/poems/45095/
sonnet-60-like-as-the-waves-make-towards-the-pebbld-shore.

as yesterday in the sight of God. Although we live from moment to moment, in the eyes of the universe, a thousand years are but as yesterday.

Five days before he died, the playwright and author William Saroyan contacted the media. These were his last public words: "I know everyone has to die, but somehow I always thought an exception would be made in my case. Now what?"

Now what? This is the urgent question of life. At some point, perhaps when we visit our alma mater decades later, we must confront our mortality. Now what? One of the most powerful urges of human beings is to master time. It is a delusion. We do not own time. Time owns us. We do not control time. Time controls us. Therefore, we must learn to make optimal use of time.

The Psalmist wrote: *The days of our years are three-score and ten—or by reason of strength—four score years. So teach us to count our days that we may acquire a heart of wisdom.*

Teach us to count our days so that we may acquire wisdom. Teach us to marvel, to express appreciation and gratitude for life itself. Teach us beauty. Teach us love, mercy, peace of mind. Teach us to laugh, and to continue to laugh until the final day. Teach us to measure our one-way journey to You with tranquility, contentment, serenity, and peace.

Before I left the campus, I spent a few moments wondering whether I could hold my own against the brilliant youngsters who study at LSE today. The university is much more selective now. I am not sure that I would even be accepted today. Still, I would like to believe that I can do things now that I couldn't do all those decades ago, and which many of the current students cannot master. I think I know better what is really important in life. I can handle failure much better. I don't get as angry with myself when I make mistakes, and I don't get as frustrated with others either. I have learned that people will disappoint you as much as they will amaze you. I know better now when to compromise. I can distinguish better between what must be taken seriously and what will simply fade away over time.

I am gratified that the Old LSE Building is still in use. There would be no New Building without the Old Building. It is still the pillar, the foundation, upon which the new emerges.

A Thousand Years
from Now

Noah lived for 350 years after the Flood...and he died.

(Genesis 9:28-29)

I date and keep everything I write. I want to remember not only what I said but when I said it. Clarity comes through context. When we are living events, we do not comprehend their long-term significance. What may seem like earth-shattering developments could turn out to be of minor importance, and what we barely paid attention to might have had decisive ramifications. Only years later, once we know how the future unfolded, can we assess our sagacity. This is true, both for individuals as well as societies in general.

Looking through files of sermons from 2019, I came across one dated 3019. Obviously it was a typo, but it got me thinking about the year 3019. What will the world look like a thousand years from now? What spectacular inventions will completely change the way humans live? Is it even possible to imagine?

A thousand years ago, in the year 1019, none of the technology we take for granted and that defines our lives was even conceivable. It is not just smart phones and computers, invented only recently, that have completely transformed how we live within a few short decades. In 1019, electricity was still 850 years away. There would be no modern plumbing, no automobiles, no air travel, no subways, no antibiotics, no anesthesia, no tall buildings, for many centuries. There was no America. Of course, there was a land mass here, with inhabitants, but in 1019, our continent was still almost 500 years from being "discovered."

A thousand years from now, when we are long gone, will our descendants regard us as we regard our ancestors from 1019, with a mixture of marvel and pity? "You mean they used to treat cancer with something called 'chemotherapy' back then?" "You mean human life spans rarely exceeded one hundred years?" "People actually traveled from place to place in something called a car, belching deadly air and noise pollution into the environment?"

In 1019, Leonardo da Vinci, the genius of the Renaissance and the precursor of the Enlightenment, was still more than 400 years from being born. The year 1019 was in the middle of what historians describe as the Middle Ages.

The middle of what? About a thousand years of nothing really important happening? The millennium separating the Byzantine period from the modern period, when Europe began to rediscover Greek and Roman philosophy, literature, and art? Imagine how we would feel today if we knew that future generations would describe our age as "Middle," to distinguish between the greatness of a previous era and the greatness of a future era.

The Bible tells us that Noah lived for 950 years. Apparently, the last 350 of them were of little historical consequence. The man who saved humanity, whose first six centuries were the most consequential imaginable, did little to merit distinction in the last third of his life. There are a few interesting tidbits about planting vineyards and drinking too much wine, but the final description of Noah reads as follows: *Noah lived after the Flood for 350 years—and then he died.*

What a profound passage! We have no idea what happened to Noah during those 350 years. The Bible seems to imply that nothing important, or worth describing, occurred during the final three and a half centuries of Noah's life. It was the middle age between the Flood and Abraham.

After Noah's death, the Bible describes the line of his descendants, one by one, verse after verse, until reaching Abraham. Abraham represents the renaissance of the human race that had stagnated for centuries. History could now begin anew. Abraham would never have been born had it not been for the descendants of Noah, but their historical function was simply to be the bridge between one critical period and another. Not too much happened during this time that the Bible regarded as consequential.

Will our era merit a chapter in the annals of civilization? A few paragraphs? A footnote—the mere citation of our lineage that led to a new era?

How will history look at us a thousand years from now? With the same importance as we regard ourselves?

THE LILAC TREE

The years of our life are three score and ten,
or, given special strength, for score years. But
the best of them are trouble and sorrow. They
pass by speedily and we are in darkness.

(Psalm 90:10)

There is a lilac tree in Central Park that I pass every day on the way to the synagogue. To call it "a tree" is actually a stretch. It is really a bush. A bush is also an exaggeration. It is more like a shrub. It is an ugly sort of thing: short and stubby, noticeably unnoticeable, unremarkable, undistinguished, unassuming, uninspiring, uninteresting, and unbecoming. But every year, around late April or early May, the lilac tree blooms, and then, this unadorned carbuncle transforms into an exotic, aromatic wonder. You can get drunk on the scent of lilacs wafting through Central Park emanating from this indefatigable force of nature.

In the short weeks when the lilac is in full bloom, what was hardly noticeable all year becomes impossible not to notice. Hundreds of people stop and sniff, breathing in the intoxicating perfume. I live for these weeks. All winter I count down the days, peering at that ugly bush, wondering when the first buds will emerge, signaling the restoration of life. When the flowers burst open, they convey a sense of inexplicable calm, that all is well with the world. *Lo the winter is past, the blossoms appear on the earth; the flowers in bloom give off fragrance. Let me see your face; let me hear your voice; for your voice is sweet and your face is lovely.*

It doesn't get much better than this. To drink in the perfume of a lilac tree in springtime is to worship the God of life. "Little flower—but if I could understand / What you are, root and all, and all in all, / I should know what God and man is."[24]

All winter, the lilac withstands the indignities of indifference. No one stops to admire. No one stops to marvel. No one stops to notice. All winter, the lilac faces the elements alone: the bitter cold, snow, rain, darkness, and dreariness. Only the dogs pay attention; they continue to pee on its roots, no matter the weather. But all winter long, the lilac is preparing for spring. All winter, it is summoning the resources, gathering the nourishment, and timing its metamorphosis. We do not notice because it is happening below the surface.

The marvel is not the actual few weeks of blossoming. Lilacs exist for that purpose: to color the landscape for a brief moment in season. The real marvel is that such a delicate-looking creation survives the winter. In the coldest and snowiest of days, I often think to myself that the fragile lilac, nakedly exposed to the elements, will not survive. Every winter I wonder whether there will be another blossoming. But every year

---

24 Alfred Lord Tennyson, "Flower in the Crannied Wall," 1864, https://allpoetry.com/Flower-in-the-Crannied-Wall.

the lilac returns, undaunted. There is much strength inside those fragile buds. There is much beauty inside the ugly thing.

We can learn much from the lilac tree. We grow in both visible and invisible ways. The season of our blossoming is short but so sweet. The magnificence of the season depends on our capacity to withstand the harshness of the winter and the indignities of indifference. Strength emerges from adversity. Beauty is the consequence of tenacity. A lowly shrub transforms itself into one of the earth's stunning spectacles.

Winter gives meaning to the lilac tree. As long as there is life; as long as there is the potential of another growing season, the flowering of spring depends on our capacities to withstand the winter. It is darkness that gives meaning to light, fallowness that gives meaning to growth, loss that gives meaning to gain, sickness that gives meaning to health, death that gives meaning to life.

We should not yearn for permanence. Everything is transitional. Every living thing passes from this way to eternity. We seek beauty, not permanence. We measure life not by the length of the growing season, but by the richness of its colors. The season of the lilac's blossoming is but a few short weeks. If the lilac tree were in full bloom all year round, after a while, no one would notice. It is the brevity of the blossoming season and the rarity of the sight that moves us so profoundly. If everything stayed the same, if the tree was always in bloom, it would lose the power to enchant us. The most precious thing in life is impermanence. The most interesting thing in life is contrast. The most certain thing in life is uncertainty.

Therefore, we pray not for certainty, but for strength. We pray for the ability to endure and for the capacity to anticipate renewal even in the winters of our discontent. We learn from the lilac tree that variety is the spice of life, change is the fact of life, and mortality is the price of life.

We should not pray for sameness. When every day is the same, when every experience is the same, when winter is just winter, not a preparation for spring—it signals that we are approaching the end of the natural cycle. At some point, there will be a final season of growth, a final spring, even for the lilac tree.

I often visit residents of assisted living facilities. The very old know that the end of life is approaching. They know there will be no springtime renewal. Every day is the same for the residents. They are waiting, but not for another growing season. Sameness is what characterizes the last winter. On one visit, I entered the common room. The television was on, but no one was watching. An old man in a wheelchair intoned, "Look at what has become of me. I was a soldier. I am a veteran. No one listens anymore." I do not know to whom he was talking; maybe to no one, but he spoke to me. No one listens. No one pays attention. The world passes by. The very elderly share the same fate as the tree in winter, but without the hope of the regeneration of spring. It is the indignity of indifference without the next cycle.

Thus, we learn a final lesson from the lilac tree: The season is short. Stop and smell the flowers. Yes, there are tasks we must do. There are responsibilities to address. But we should not spend our entire lives laboring, planting, and preparing for the next season. We should enjoy this season too.

There is a special prayer mentioned in the Talmud that I think of upon seeing the first flowers of the lilac tree:

> Praised are you O God, Ruler of the Universe, Who did not leave anything lacking in the world, and created in it good creatures and good trees to give pleasure to human beings.

MORTALITY

There is a season for everything, a time
for every experience under heaven: A
time to be born and a time to die.

(Ecclesiastes 3:1-2)

J orge Luis Borges wrote a short story called "The Immortal."
It is about a Roman solider, Marcus Rufus, who searched
the world for the fabled river of immortality. Finding it,
he drinks the waters and becomes immortal. Borges described
the Immortals as not much interested in their own fate. Since
they never die, they did not bother to take care of their bodies. All they needed were a few hours' sleep each month, a
little water, and a scrap of meat. Borges writes, "I recall [an
Immortal] whom I never saw standing—a bird had made its
nest on his breast." Since the body never died, it had minimal
needs, and the Immortals ultimately denigrated the body in
favor of the mind. They were all contemplation, all thought,
with little attention to physical needs or enjoyment.

Borges wrote: "There is nothing very remarkable about
being immortal; with the exception of mankind, all creatures
are immortal, for they know nothing of death. What is divine,
terrible, and incomprehensible is to know oneself immortal."

What a magnificent thought: knowledge of mortality defines mortality. Every living thing except us lacks consciousness of death. Death does not terrorize those who have no knowledge of it. To be unaware of mortality is to be immortal. Awareness of mortality is what terrifies us. Borges suggests that only humans seek immortality because only humans comprehend the concept of death. But when Rufus becomes immortal, the knowledge that he will never die terrifies him.

Here is the tragic irony of the human creature. More than anything, we want to live. But living forever, even more than dying, is the ultimate terror. "Everything in the world of mortals has the value of the irrecoverable and contingent," Borges wrote. "Among the immortals, on the other hand…nothing is preciously in peril of being lost." Therefore, none of the actions of the Immortals has any significance whatsoever. All are unimportant because over an infinitely long period of time, all things happen to all people. There are no spiritual or intellectual merits.

The point of being alive is the knowledge that there are consequences that are contingent and irrecoverable. If nothing is in peril of being lost, nothing is at stake. And if nothing is at stake, what is the point of life? It was this sense that nothing is at stake that propelled Rufus to search the world for the river that would undo his immortality. He concluded that if he never died, there was no reason for living. He did not want to be immortal. Immortality was a burden, not a release. Never dying meant never really living. Rufus found peace only when he restored his mortality. The very mortality we dread is what gives life urgency, poignancy, and a dimension of eternality.

The rabbis of the Talmud made the same point. They described the mythical city of Luz. While the powerful conquerors of the ancient world—Sennacherib and Nebuchadnezzar—invaded other cities, killing and exiling their inhabitants, they spared Luz—perhaps because precious and prized sky-blue wool was produced there. Even the angel of death had no permission to enter. There was no dislocation, no upheaval, and no death in Luz. Nonetheless, once the elderly decided that they reached the end of life, they walked outside the city wall and died. Although they could have lived forever, the people of Luz voluntarily rejected immortality.

Our lives have meaning because they are finite.

Happiness

You have put happiness in my heart.

(Psalms 4:8-9)

The most popular course in the history of Yale is on happiness. The university scrambles to find lecture halls large enough to contain all the eager students.

What is missing in the lives of our young people? What worries them? Why this fixation on happiness at such a budding age? Yale students are among the most gifted and privileged humans who ever walked the face of the Earth. If anyone should be happy, it is them. Yet administrators and faculty members perceive deep dissatisfaction within their student bodies. They point to a burgeoning mental health crisis on campuses across America. How can we explain that even before their careers begin, before the grind, the children, the mortgages, the professional setbacks, the financial stress—that even during this tender teenage time, they pine for that elusive elixir of life that has baffled and befuddled all those who came before them? What is it about our era that creates such discontent among even the youngest, most capable, and privileged of us?

Technically, the students at Yale register for a science class called "Positive Psychology." This is the scientific study of positive human functioning and flourishing: the scientific study of the factors contributing to a well-lived and meaningful life. In 21st century America, we assume that science can solve every problem, even the age-old dilemma of happiness. Positive human functioning and flourishing were traditionally the domain of the humanities, but these departments struggle to stay open at most colleges because students want to be engineers, software developers, and business graduates. It is as if even the study of ethics, morals, and values needs a scientific sheen to attract ambitious, career-oriented young adults. Heaven forbid that these future masters of the universe waste their time on philosophy, literature, or religion.

Still, if it takes the veneer of science to entice our most brilliant to contemplate a well-lived and meaningful life, count me in.

Leaders in the field of positive psychology cite studies that conclude there is a very low correlation between material wealth and happiness, except in cases of extreme poverty, where people's basic needs are not met. They point to research that indicates as countries grow wealthier, there is no increase in levels of happiness. In fact, often, happiness decreases. Some people are actually more depressed when they come into money. It ruins their lives. Happiness scientists conclude that "[we] didn't realize this in the same way ten years ago, that our intuitions about what will make us happy, like winning the lottery, are totally wrong."

Wow! What an earth-shattering scientific discovery!

Nearly three millennia ago, Ecclesiastes wrote: *A lover of money never has his fill of money. It is futile. He must depart just as he came. Naked he arrived and naked he leaves. What real value is there—in all the gains and riches one makes?* When it comes to money, famed journalist and writer H.L. Mencken, not a brain specialist but a master observer of the human heart, captured the essence of human emotions better than any Positive Psychologist: "A [happy] man is one who earns $100 a year more than his wife's sister's husband."

In the Yale course, students are required to perform acts of kindness and form new social connections, described as "rewirement" assignments.

Wow! I love this rewiring. Two thousand seven hundred years ago, the prophet Hosea said: *I rewired them with cords of human kindness, with bands of love. My heart is turned within me, my compassion is kindled.*

There is an element of hubris in the assertion that scientists, not humanists, have finally discovered the secret to happiness. It is about rewiring our brain. If we can stimulate our prefrontal cortex to produce more electrical impulses, we will be happy. Soon, we will invent a drug that will activate the left prefrontal cortices of people who have deficiencies there, and when we feel unhappy, we will just pop a happiness pill in the morning and slake our never-ending thirst for the elixir of life.

Finally, eternal bliss within our grasp, courtesy of big pharma.

Americans are healthier and safer than previous generations. We live much longer. Yet, we seem tenser, angrier, less secure, and less happy. Why?

Jean-Jacques Rousseau suggested that our greater progress causes our greater unhappiness. That modernity, itself, robs us of what we need to be happy, undermining religious faith, disrupting community, and sapping our courage, decency, and virtue. Technologically advanced civilizations sever people from each other, and eventually, from themselves. Rousseau contended that modern Man is a shell of his true self. We are our own worst enemies. "In learning to desire, we have made ourselves the slaves of our desires," he wrote.

We have come to believe that to realize ourselves we must focus exclusively on ourselves. In Oscar Wilde's *The Picture of Dorian Gray*, Lord Henry said to Dorian:

> The aim of life is self-development. To realize one's nature perfectly—that is what each of us is here for. People...have forgotten the highest of all duties, the duty that one owes to one's self. Of course they are charitable. They feed the hungry, and clothe the beggar. But their own souls starve, and are naked.

Dorian Gray eventually self-destructed. We cannot long endure, attractive on the outside but ugly on the inside, beautiful in body but deformed in spirit. Of course, we must nourish the body. We must cultivate the best of ourselves, exercising the full use of our powers along the lines of excellence. But life is not only about the self. We need others. The human spirit responds to, and is strengthened by, goodness, kindness, social connections, family, and friends. The Yale Positive Psychology course emphasizes these values too, the very ones that the Bible urged already millennia ago.

It is not that modern science sprinted ahead of religion in understanding happiness. Rather, science has finally caught up with religion, agreeing with and validating it. The greatest of our species have been urging us to rewire our brains for eons. They insisted on performing acts of kindness, becoming accustomed—habituated—to moral, magnanimous, and merciful deeds. They realized that the more we do, the more we accept the need for doing. Habits and routines influence philosophy. Jewish sages emphasized that what may have started out as an act without understanding, over time, generates understanding. The habit of giving charity eventually changes the way we feel about charity.

In other words, we are rewired.

Judaism teaches that God placed us in a world of unending challenges. Over and over, our tradition reminded us that, for one reason or another, and for better or for worse, God created the world imperfect; a world that needs improvement. Our task is to improve ourselves—but not only ourselves. The individual and society are interconnected, woven together in a common thread of fate. "If I am not for myself, who will be for me," Hillel the Elder taught. "But if I am only for myself, what am I?" Goodness never desires itself. Its aim is always outside of the self—someone else. The soul must free itself from itself.

The way to improve is to contend. We get better through struggle. If we define happiness as the absence of struggle, we will never be happy. Judaism teaches that there is no such thing as a life without struggle. It is an illusion—snake oil. We are sold delusional visions of happiness that are inconsistent with the nature of the universe and our own nature. If we are honest with ourselves, we do not really want a world without struggle. Life would be boring. Adversity brings out the best in us. And in any case, we cannot possess perpetual bliss. Problems beget problems. They never end. No sooner have you resolved one problem, a host of additional problems arise.

Happiness cannot mean attainment. We are bound to fall short. We always end our journey on this side of the river, the Promised Land glimpsed only in the distant horizon. The struggle, not the fulfillment, defines us. Our goal is to live in creative tension, our grasp constantly exceeding our reach. Movement, not rest, is the goal of life. Lack of movement is death. We have a term for it: Rest in Peace. Motion is the propellant of life.

When we speak of happiness, we mean a deep-seated contentment, a sense of satisfaction and gratitude in living purposeful and meaningful lives. We pay a huge price if we assume that the purpose of life is limited only to the improvement of the self—a price that Yale undergraduates already recognize in their future selves. Our form may prosper, but our soul will wither. The body may be happy, but the spirit will be miserable. We may have fat wallets but thin purpose. We will end up constantly asking ourselves, "Is this all there is to life?" The American founding fathers spoke of the "pursuit of happiness." The pursuit more than the overtaking, the anticipation more than the realization, give excitement and meaning.

Robert Louis Stevenson wrote:

It is true that we shall never reach the goal; it is even more probable that there is no such place; and if we lived for centuries and were endowed with the powers of a god, we should find ourselves not much nearer what we wanted at the end. O toiling hands of mortals! O unwearied feet, traveling ye know not wither! Soon, soon, it seems to you, you must come forth on some conspicuous hilltop, and but a little way further, against the setting sun, descry the spires of El Dorado. Little do ye know your own blessedness; for to travel hopefully is a better thing than to arrive, and the true success is to labour.

MONEY

When you have eaten your fill and have built fine
houses to live in...and your silver and gold have
increased, and everything you own has prospered,
beware lest your heart grow haughty...

(Deuteronomy 8:14)

Judaism is not conflicted about money. We acknowledge
the healthy appetites of human beings. We are commanded to take pleasure in the world and to delight in the
beneficence of God's universe. *When one eats and drinks and*
derives enjoyment out of his wealth, it is a gift of God. People
should work hard and earn a good living. Moreover, our tradition emphasizes that there are many social problems that can
be solved only through affluence.

Jews are not attracted to poverty. Poverty is no virtue.
We do not take oaths of poverty. There is nothing inherently
noble in poverty. A poor person is not necessarily honorable,
and an honorable person is not necessarily poor. For the most
part, Judaism considered poverty to be pointless suffering.
The sages warned: "There is nothing worse than poverty. If all
the suffering and pain in the world were gathered on one side
of the scale and poverty was on the other side, poverty would

outweigh them all." A healthy bank account is preferable to counting pennies. Independence is better than dependence. Giving charity is better than receiving charity.

We do not equate limited financial assets with abundant spiritual assets. A full religious life does not require an empty material life. The assertion that "it is easier for a camel to go through the eye of a needle than for a rich man to enter into the kingdom of God" is not a Jewish idea. It appears to us, actually, quite unrealistic and disconnected from the human psyche.

Judaism acknowledges that financial security is critical to our welfare. It is impossible to focus on higher thoughts when we are hungry, thirsty, homeless, or in pain. As Shakespeare wrote, "There was never yet [a] philosopher [who] could endure the toothache." We attain wellbeing of the soul only after securing wellbeing of the body, Maimonides taught. Contemporary mental health experts confirm that severe financial pressure is detrimental to our health and can lead to illness and even death.

Therefore, piety for Jews does not require abstinence. We do not believe in mortification, the denial of our body's needs, or in monasticism, the denial of our social needs. Our holy men and women did not withdraw from the world. We do not aspire to deprivation nor do we feel guilty about financial success. The opposite: we admire people who have prospered by virtue of their own honest efforts. Judaism never denigrated wealth. To the contrary, the Talmud states that we will be called to account in the next world for all of the legitimate pleasures we have denied ourselves in this world.

However, the sages cautioned that our appetites are often more powerful than our convictions: that wealth, and the pursuit of wealth, often lead to haughtiness and injustice. Therefore, when it comes to money, Judaism insists on both external and internal regulation.

First, and foremost, we must produce our wealth through honest means. "To rob a person even of the value of a [penny] is like taking his life away," proclaim the sages. It is impermissible to steal, even to give to the less fortunate. Robin Hood was not a Jew. We cannot take what is not ours for any purpose. The Talmud points out that the generation of the flood was not doomed until they stretched out their hands to steal.

Moreover, "Thou shalt not steal" is both a personal commandment and a social obligation. A system of unjust laws; an economy that reeks of cheating, not merit, where the overall impression is that the game is rigged and that only a few are in on the secret, is a society on the precipice. We often separate economic calculus from moral calculus, but morally sound economic policies are the key to a decent society. Policies that contribute to or tolerate poverty are contrary to the spirit of religion. They suppress the image of God and contribute to the eclipse of human dignity.

Our obligations are not limited to following the letter of the law. The medieval commentator Nachmanides pointed out that someone who observes only the letter of the law can easily become a scoundrel with the permission of the law. We can take improper financial advantage of people without breaking the law. We can mislead people without breaking the law. We can be cold and arrogant, cruel and selfish, without breaking the law. It is possible to stiff your employees legally.

An honorable person hates misleading others, even if it is legal. We read in the Talmud of Rabbi Shimon ben Shetach, who bought a donkey from a gentile farmer. When his servants brought it home, they found a precious gem in the harness. The rabbi immediately ordered his servants to return the gem because he only intended to purchase the donkey not the jewel, proclaiming, "I would prefer that a gentile say, 'blessed be the God of the Jews' than all of the money in the world."

An honorable person abhors exploiting others, even if it is legal. An honorable person is troubled by having more than enough while others have nowhere near enough, even though it is legal. An honorable person is motivated not only by what is profitable, but also by what is prophetic: integrity, honesty, reputability, and reliability are as important to him as profitability. An honorable person is driven not only by valuations, but by values. It is not all about bank accounts; it is also about accountability.

It is not all about money. It is also about mercy.

Second, if we have affluence, we must share it. It is a commandment, an obligation, not a choice. We are required to give to the less fortunate. It is a matter of justice. All human beings, created in God's image, are equally entitled to human dignity. It is obscene that some have so much that they cannot figure out what to do with all their money, while others do not have enough to put food on the table. Something about our contemporary culture blinds us to our responsibility to those who have little or nothing. Few of us pause on our upwardly mobile climb to look down at humanity below. How many of us truly care about the struggles of others? We are often oblivious to anyone but ourselves.

Third, at some point we must conclude that we have enough. The sage Ben Zoma asks, "Who is rich?" He responds, "One who is happy with what he has." We are creatures of desire. No matter how much we have, we always want more. We are never satisfied. *The eye never has its fill of seeing.* Therefore, Jewish sages teach that our most valuable possessions are often those least financially valuable.

There is a passage in the Talmud about a flute in the Temple that was delicate, smooth, fine, and made of simple reed that dated back to the days of Moses himself. The king issued an order to plate the flute with gold, and its sound was no longer pleasant. They then removed the gold and the sound was as pleasing as before.

Money does not improve everything. Some people who came into enormous wealth saw it destroy what was most important to them. After all, even if we have every material possession we ever dreamed of, if we are not happy with what we have, what is the point of having it?

As Maurice Sendak wrote: "There must be more to life than having everything."

FAILURE

As soon as Moses came near the camp and saw
the calf and the dancing, he became enraged,
and hurled the tablets from his hands, shattering
them at the foot of the mountain.

(Exodus 32:19)

Failure intrigues me.

People often forget that failure is a necessary ingredient of success. Our natural tendency is to admire accomplished people at their moment of triumph. Rarely do we inquire how many times they failed before they succeeded. "Into each life some rain must fall," Longfellow wrote. "Some days must be dark and dreary." Americans do not respond well to dark and dreary. We are a sunny people. We venerate success. We consider failure practically un-American. We worship winners. Winning brings glory. Losing is unbearable.

Actually, we lose much more often than we win. All of us lose. All of us lose all the time. We fail more than we succeed. It is why winning is so empowering and intoxicating. Losing is more common. In head-to-head competition, there is only one winner. Only one political candidate wins an election. Her opponent loses. The loss is not necessarily permanent.

There are future battles to be won. But this competition was lost. Another candidate got the job I wanted. Only one student finished first in the class.

Jewish tradition accepts failure as a necessary part of life. We fail in the big things and we fail in the little things. We fall short on our most promising ambitions. "Oft expectation fails," wrote Shakespeare, "and most oft, there, where most it promises."

Much of the Torah focuses on our people's shortcomings, described in exquisite and painful detail. Our ignominy is in full view. Every patriarch and matriarch is flawed. No biblical figure is without blemish, even Moses. More times than not, the Torah describes the people of Israel backsliding, disappointing themselves, their leaders, and God. The Ten Commandments are, perhaps, our people's most profound accomplishment. We often forget that it followed the most depraved failure in Jewish history, the worship of the Golden Calf. The Ten Commandments were the result of another try, our second effort. Moses shattered the original tablets. Such was his horror and disgust. How refreshing that a holy book makes no effort to hide the blemishes of even its greatest heroes. The Torah's honesty enhances its credibility. Success is not the absence of flaws, but overcoming our flaws; not how many times we fell, but how many times we got up. Even the best of us fall—and fall often.

J.K. Rowling delivered a brilliant commencement address at Harvard University in 2008, entitled "The Fringe Benefits of Failure." Rowling, who sold more books than any author in our time, was once, as she described in her speech, "as poor as it is possible to be in modern Britain, without being homeless." She said about herself: "By any conventional measure, a mere seven years after my graduation day, I had failed on an epic scale. An exceptionally short-lived marriage had imploded, and I was jobless…. The fears my parents had had for me, and that I had had for myself, had both come to pass, and by every usual standard, I was the biggest failure I knew."

This completely self-made woman was disappointed time after time. Her manuscript was rejected over and over again. So-called successful people, executives of major publishing houses, were unable to see the potential of this impoverished woman.

What did Rowling learn, and what did she advise the Harvard graduates?

> What I feared most for myself…was not poverty, but failure…. Now, I am not going to stand here and tell you that failure is fun. That period of my life was a dark one…. I had no idea how far the tunnel extended, and for a long time, any light at the end of it was a hope rather than a reality.
>
> So why do I talk about the benefits of failure? Simply because failure meant a stripping away of the inessential. I stopped pretending to myself that I was anything other than what I was, and began to direct all my energy into finishing the only work that mattered to me. Had I really succeeded at anything else, I might never have found the determination to succeed in the one arena I believed I truly belonged. I was set free,

because my greatest fear had already been realized, and I was still alive, and I still had a daughter whom I adored, and I had an old typewriter and a big idea. And so, rock bottom became the solid foundation on which I rebuilt my life....

Failure gave me an inner security that I had never attained by passing examinations. Failure taught me things about myself that I could have learned no other way.... You will never truly know yourself, or the strength of your relationships, until both have been tested by adversity. Such knowledge is a true gift, for all that it is painfully won, and it has been worth more than any qualification I ever earned....

Some failure in life is inevitable. It is impossible to live without failing at something, unless you live so cautiously that you might as well not have lived at all—in which case, you fail by default.

This is profound, even biblical, wisdom. Success is the result of failure. There can be no accomplishment, no grand achievement, without multiple failures. Success in life is persistence: in our capacity to overcome our faults, flaws, and failings. *A righteous man falls down seven times—and gets up—while the unworthy are tripped up by one misfortune.*

We cannot succeed if we do not fail. In the words of Winston Churchill, who was well acquainted with failure:

"Success is going from failure to failure without loss of enthusiasm."

Stroke of Insight

*My soul cries for You, O God. My soul
thirsts for God, the living God.*

(Psalm 42:2-3)

Moses would have been a flop on modern television. He either had a speech impediment, or at the very least, felt inarticulate and tongue-tied. His every mispronounced word, every eruption of anger, would have been played and replayed on social media, and looped on twenty-four-hour cable news channels. And forget prophets like Isaiah, Jeremiah, or Ezekiel. They might be derided today as fringe personalities at best, and at worst, wild-eyed lunatics. Even in their own days, many considered these prophetic geniuses unhinged.

Why?

I read a short fascinating book entitled *My Stroke of Insight*, by Jill Bolte Taylor. She is a Harvard-trained neuroanatomist who, at the age of thirty-seven, suffered a massive hemorrhagic stroke on the left side of her brain. In the book, she described in detail her experiences, from the moment of her episode through the many years of recovery. She could examine the effect of stroke, as she described, "from the inside out," as a scientist observing herself.

She described how her stroke incapacitated the left hemisphere of her brain, the side that controls language. The left hemisphere focuses on the past. It is oriented toward achievement. We define, organize, and categorize information in the left hemisphere. It is the side of ego and rationality. It controls judgment. It sets limits. It is in-the-box thinking. Much of this part of her personality was lost on that morning when Taylor suffered her stroke.

Her right hemisphere, however, was not damaged. The right part of the brain thinks in pictures. Joy exists in the right hemisphere. Taylor described how colors became much bolder and more vivid. She could appreciate music as never before; she could even sing on key for the first time in her life. She felt more compassion, observed more beauty, saw more curves and textures than ever before. Her creativity blossomed.

She wrote that now she felt a deep inner peace, an inexplicable but very real feeling. She felt connected to the source of energy in the universe. She felt at one with the universe and could appreciate her life's meaning as part of something much grander and much more awesome. She wrote that when she lost capacity in her left hemisphere, the right hemisphere became uninhibited. It was freed from the self-restricting, self-defining, rationality-based, judgmental, in-the-box thinking of her left hemisphere.

Taylor's experience revealed to her an aspect of existence that is so powerful, so dazzling, so overwhelming, so laden with meaning, and so reality-based, that she, a driven, brilliant Harvard-trained scientist, would have never understood this aspect of human existence had she not had her episode.

Taylor did not address religion in her book. I think that she never even mentioned the word "God." Still, I found her observations to be deeply spiritual—an effort to probe the source of existence and to understand the purpose of life. I thought of all those spiritual geniuses—not the Newtons, Einsteins, and Galileos of the world whose left-hemisphere capacities were enormous, but rather people like Isaiah, Jeremiah, Ezekiel, Amos, Mozart, Beethoven, Chopin, Leonardo, Michelangelo, Shakespeare—these geniuses of the spirit—who must have had stronger right-hemisphere capacities that allowed them to see and feel what others could not. They could tap into what Taylor described as the source of energy in the universe and observe spiritual vistas with greater clarity. They could penetrate better the secret of existence, and there, if they thought in religious categories, could understand better what we call the presence of God.

Of course, we cannot exist with any independence without our left hemisphere. We would be unable to care for ourselves, nor would we be able to reason and rationalize or advance scientifically and technologically. But what Taylor emphasized is that the right hemisphere is also part of our makeup, and allows us to access a reality of the universe that is mostly inaccessible. This could explain why some people feel so powerfully and personally the reality of God in their lives, while others deem such people delusional, psychotic, unhinged, or in pursuit of some God idea that seems to them entirely irrational and childish.

Taylor concludes that we simply do not engage the skills of our right hemispheres enough. She said that she estimates that 85 percent of our thoughts are left-hemisphere centered, and at most, only 15 percent are right-hemisphere centered. Not only do we not engage our right hemisphere enough, she argued, but we actually mock those who do. We say to people, "Stop day-dreaming and solve that equation." She wrote, "I realized that deep internal peace is accessible to anyone at any time…. All we have to do is silence the voice of our dominating left mind."

As that genius of the right hemisphere once put it:

"There are more things in heaven and earth, Horatio, / Than are dreamt of in your philosophy."[25]

---

25 William Shakespeare, *Hamlet*, 1.5.187-188,
    https://www.folger.edu/hamlet.

THE DARK SIDE

Most devious is the heart; it is
perverse—who can fathom it?

(Jeremiah 17:9)

I have been a rabbi for thirty-four years. Our vocation is devoted to building up, not tearing down. Rabbis are the repository of thousands of years of learning about and observing human nature. We think about good and bad, right and wrong, honesty and dishonesty, honor and dishonor, all the time. We try to teach, model proper behavior, and avoid improper acts.

But the rabbinate, too, can be a nursery of ambition. Every calling has potentates and aspirants clinging to the skirts of authority. The Talmud is filled with descriptions of mean-spirited competitiveness, un-satiated ambition, scathing insults, and raw envy among the Sages. There is no attempt to hide the simmering volcano of visceral emotions that live in all of us, including role models of ethical behavior. In our times, too, I have observed a kind of ecclesiastical ego that belies avowals of modesty. I have witnessed levels of cutthroat competition no different from any other occupation. "Who knows how easily ambition disguises itself under the name of a calling," wrote Victor Hugo, "possibly in good faith and deceiving itself, in sanctimonious confusion?"

No clergy, from the highest clerical figure to the humblest neighborhood pastor, is exempt from the dark side of human nature, because we, ourselves, are human.

Human beings are such a piece of work. We are merciful. We practice friendship. We give and receive love. Yet often, darkness eclipses our splendor. We are capable of admiration and envy at the same time. We can express compassion and ego in the same act. We may be charitable and uncharitable in one fell swoop. For every noble impulse in us, it seems that an equal and opposite impulse pulls us down. Plato equated the human condition to that of a charioteer whose horses pull in different directions. We try to ride the right road of life, but these wild stallions of our personality keep pulling us in opposite directions. A fierce struggle rages inside each of us, an unrelenting civil war between our competing inclinations.

All of us know people who are doing well but cannot be content if their neighbor is doing well. They feel less accomplished because other people have larger homes, larger bank accounts, or larger cars. They are doing fine in their careers, but someone is doing better. It drives them to distraction. Such people often lift themselves up by tearing you down. They gossip, they lie, they make things up. They magnify and distort your flaws and magnify and distort their talents. When you are successful, they will envy; when you fail, they will rejoice; when you struggle, they will be content.

This is the stuff of human life. Such *a twisted thing cannot be made straight, a lack that cannot be made good.* The

Rabbis called our propensity for virtue *yetzer hatov*, "the good impulse," and our inclination for corruption *yetzer hara*, "the bad impulse."

Jewish tradition never sought to deny our problematic side. The sages taught that this, too, is part of the human condition. Every twinge of envy we feel when someone else is recognized is hardwired into our system. God made us this way. It is one of the central contentions of Judaism. We learn from the first chapter of the Bible that the totality of the human creature is good. Even our negative drives can be good. Ambition, competitiveness, ego, profit—these are what push us to achieve, excel, and propel human progress. The sages were skeptical that altruism alone would be a powerful enough motive for hard work, success, and invention.

For example, unlike other religious philosophies that consider ambition, pride, and sex to be sinful, the rabbis taught that without these, no one would write great books, build beautiful houses, or even raise families. Anyone who writes books understands that part of the allure is not only the good impulse of sharing your thoughts with others. Authors also write books because they want to see their name on the cover. They want to be relevant, talked about, and important. Architects build ever more stunning houses, and owners commission ever more creative architects, because they want to build and showcase a structure that will impress others. Carnal drives produce the next generation.

Judaism asserts that ego, self-regard, and self-interest propel achievement and progress. Contemporary mental health experts confirm that self-esteem and a high sense of self-worth are healthy. Those who have low self-respect are less likely to perform at a high level in society and are less likely to be satisfied.

The desire for recognition pushes us to succeed. Jews are honest in this regard. Our tradition did not attempt to hide the reality of our ego or excuse it. We believe that for practically all of us there is no such thing as pure and utter selflessness. Human beings were not designed that way. We enter this world yapping and shrieking for attention. Babies are attention-sucking machines. We never lose this craving for attention. We like being the best. We seek praise. We want to be respected, recognized, and honored.

The rabbis taught that our goal is not to eliminate our problematic inclination. To deny our "dark side" is to deny ourselves. On its face, this side of our personality is not even dark. It is neutral—simply who we are. It becomes undesirable through excess, by our inability to control ourselves. The sage Ben Zoma, asked, "Who is strong?" He responded, "One who masters his impulses."

Judaism teaches that we can increasingly master our problematic impulses through fortitude, self-control, and self-discipline. "If one desires to turn himself to the path of good and be righteous, the choice is his," Maimonides wrote. "Should he desire to turn to the path of evil and be wicked, the choice is his." "The devil made me do it" is no excuse in Jewish tradition. If we are unable to restrain ambition, ego, envy, lust, attraction, hunger for power, they will grow stronger and eventually destroy us. It is a constant, daily struggle. Rabbi Isaac said, "A person's Evil Desire renews itself daily against him…. It grows stronger within him from day to day." "At first," the sages taught, "it is like the thread of a spider, but ultimately becomes like cart ropes."

The negative impulse lures us, entrapping us in a deadly web, drawing us ineluctably inward. We become subservient to our emotions—slaves of passion—rather than in control of our destiny. If we do not exercise dominion over ourselves, we will be straightjacketed, trapped, within the devices of our own making. Only when we have mastered ourselves can we say that we are truly free.

The rabbis insisted that we can prevail against ourselves. They explain:

> One day, the Holy One will bring the evil inclination before the righteous and the wicked. To the righteous, it will have the appearance of a towering hill; and to the wicked, it will have the appearance of a strand of hair. Both the righteous and the wicked will weep. The righteous will weep saying, "How were we able to overcome such a towering hill?" The wicked will weep saying: "How is it that we were unable to overcome this strand of hair?"

The human being is a dangerous creature when out of control. The greater the person, the greater the *yetzer*, the sages taught. The best of us, the most successful, the most ambitious, the most talented, tend to be those who have the most powerful inclinations and the most intense internal struggles. That is why so many who have reached the top of their fields come crashing down in scandal. Their powerful impulses—the very attributes that propelled them to the top of the heap—eventually get the better of them.

The rabbis do not simply describe the problem. They offer a solution. The Talmud states: "The Holy One spoke unto Israel: 'My children, I created the evil impulse—but I also created the Torah as its antidote. If you occupy yourselves with Torah, you will not be delivered into the hands of the evil impulse.'" The school of Rabbi Ishmael taught: "If this repulsive wretch meets you, drag him to the House of Study."

It is a classic Jewish approach. What is the method to deal with our daily struggle to control ourselves? Study and reflection. We converse with, and gain access to, the greatest minds of history. We come to understand that we are not alone. All human beings struggle with the same impulses. We can overcome. We can master our straying hearts and our self-absorbed minds. We can do it by learning how others have done it.

We do not seek to eliminate the joy of food, but to control our appetite. We do not seek to eliminate the joy of wine, but to control our sobriety. We do not seek to eliminate our acquisition of material resources—poverty is not a virtue in Judaism—but to find balance between consuming and sharing. Enjoy food, but don't be a glutton. Enjoy wine, but don't be a drunk. Be ambitious, but don't be an egomaniac. Influence others, but don't be authoritarian. Lead, but don't be a tyrant.

There is a concept in Jewish thought called "a fence around the Torah." We protect ourselves from violating a core prohibition by creating a peripheral obstacle—a fence. If we cannot surmount the fence, we cannot violate the core prohibition.

For example, to reduce the risk of taking the name of God in vain, the rabbis advised not to swear oaths at all. In this way, one did not run the risk of swearing falsely.

The sages advise avoiding even the first step on the wrong path, because it may be impossible to resist the next step. It is the first wrong steps that count, wrote Mark Twain. Odysseus ordered his men to tie him to the mast as their ship passed the island of the sirens. Even he, the commander of men, could not command himself to resist the temptation of the siren song. He knew that even one alluring note could lead to his downfall.

The key is to know yourself and to overcome your impulses. We can do it. We know what is right and what is wrong. We do not need clergy, therapists, attorneys, philosophers, and moralists to tell us. We know on our own. If we build a fence around our weaknesses, if we establish disciplines that will prevent our negative impulses from being overly activated, we will better protect ourselves. The more one yields to one's passions, the more mastery they gain over him.

In frequent moments of disappointment with the problematic passions of the ordained, often no weaker—and sometimes stronger—than the passions of the un-ordained, I remind myself of a 19th and 20th century giant of the rabbinate, Yisrael Kagan, better known as The Chafetz Chayim, who lived to the ripe age of ninety-five. When he was already very old, he was asked how he managed still to get up so early every day. He responded:

"When I wake up I tell myself that my *yetzer* is also very old—as old as I am—and he has already arisen, and so must I."

The Broad Heart

And God endowed King Solomon with intelligence,
and with very much wisdom, and with a broad
heart—a heart as vast as the sands on the seashore.

(I Kings 5:9)

I led a synagogue delegation to Poland in April 2022. For weeks I had watched from the safe confines of my living room as the Russian military had mauled millions of innocent civilians in an unprovoked, unjustified, unconscionable, unrestrained, merciless, and savage invasion. I was inexpressibly frustrated by simply watching. I wanted our synagogue to do something—for Ukrainians—but also for ourselves.

We are morally diminished if all we do is bemoan orgies of atrocities from afar, lamenting all manner of human perversities while downing the last sips of our morning repast. Synagogues aspire not merely to be critics. We want to be actors, messengers of mercy, co-workers of kindness, consolation, and comfort, representing and expressing the best of Jewish values.

We raised hundreds of thousands of dollars to support aid workers and humanitarian organizations. We brought 1,200 pounds of supplies with us, everything from undergarments, to toiletries, medicines, and hygiene products. And most importantly, we brought compassion and kindness to Ukrainians who had lost everything.

We saw hundreds of refugees. At the Ukrainian border, we stood by busloads of broken, shell-shocked human beings disembarking from their harrowing journey, finally free of Russian terror. In Warsaw and Krakow, we interacted with refugees who were just beginning to grapple with their new reality: they would not be returning to their homes or their former lives anytime soon, if ever.

One encounter in Krakow reduced me to tears. We entered a giant warehouse, established in haste from a converted shopping mall. Mountains of clothes, donated from every part of the globe, were offered to any person who entered the facility. No money was exchanged. Ukrainian refugees simply took what they needed. Dresses, shirts, pants, underwear, socks, shoes, were neatly arranged according to style and size. If you didn't know the tragic background, this place would seem like any thrift shop in the West. That was the point: to provide not only basic necessities, but to offer as much dignity and compassion as possible. It reminded me of the stories I heard from my mother, who spent months in the DP camp of Bergen-Belsen after the war. Camp officials made a concerted effort to restore basic dignity to survivors, as quickly and as comprehensively as possible. Traumatized and dehumanized women were offered fine clothes of the latest European fashion, cosmetics, perfumes, and hair stylists, so they could feel themselves coming back to themselves.

We spent forty-five minutes in the warehouse. But it was only when we were outside that I was overwhelmed with emotion. We arrived first thing in the morning. By the time we left, a long line had formed. They were almost all women and children. Men between the ages of eighteen and sixty were prevented from leaving Ukraine.

I looked deeply at these suffering souls who had lost everything. Feelings of utter helplessness overwhelmed me. All these millions of people suddenly rendered refugees, all this suffering—it was caused by one man, Vladimir Putin. He decided to launch this brutal assault. For sure, he was enabled by many others, but the invasion of Ukraine would not have happened if Putin didn't want it to happen.

It is astonishing to me how history often consigns so much power to one person. The fate of many millions was in Putin's hands. If not for him, there would be no war and no refugees.

We do not give enough consideration to the type of people who lead us. Learned experts analyze the power politics of international relations, as if there is some master algorithm that directs and constrains all leaders. Of course, there are rules to the game of thrones, but Putin's values drove his decision to invade Ukraine. His personality, life experiences, and principles led him to launch and fight the kind of war he inflicted on Ukrainians, an unrestrained, perverse all-out onslaught against civilians.

What virtues should we expect in those holding high public responsibility? The Bible raises three essential qualities granted to Solomon, considered among the greatest of the Israelite kings.

These are the virtues we seek to cultivate in ourselves as well.

INTELLIGENCE

Intelligence is important to us. We are impressed with intelligence. We are impressed with grades; we are impressed with degrees that testify to high intelligence. We rank intelligence. We prize intelligence. We honor intelligence. We recruit intelligence.

Quite right. If it is the difference between a decade in prison or freedom, we want to know how smart our attorney is. We want to know where she went to school, where she ranked, and what cases she later won. We want someone on our side who is brighter than the attorney on the other side. If it is the difference between good health and a lifetime of incapacities, we want to examine the degrees hanging on the wall of our doctor. If it is the difference between money in the bank and a life of struggle, we want to know that our financial advisor is intelligent. If it is the difference between custody of our child and splitting the baby in two, we want a judge as intellectually gifted as Solomon.

But intelligence is not enough. There are people who can whip off facts and figures practically at will: who seem to know everything about everything, but nothing more. We will never know enough. There is always more to know. The great sage Rabbi Eliezer said that while he learned much Torah, it was comparable only to what a dog laps from the lake.

Genius is a tricky thing. You might be a genius in one field, but that does not necessarily translate into other areas of life. Sigmund Freud once wrote about his conversation with Albert Einstein: "He understands as much about psychology as I do about physics, so we had a very pleasant talk." Plenty of people are truly brilliant, the smartest in the class by far, but the dumbest in life. They are described as the best and the brightest but turn out to be best at what is not bright and bright at what is not best. Plenty of people can solve the crossword puzzle swiftly but cannot navigate the crossroads of life even slowly. They can answer every clue on *Jeopardy!* but have no clue how to avoid putting themselves in jeopardy.

It is a shame that the most evil are not the least intelligent. Some people attended the best colleges in the world but did the worst deeds. I will never forget the strange tale of the Christmas Day Bomber who tried to bring down a Detroit-bound plane in 2009. He received the moniker "The Underwear Bomber," because he smuggled the bomb inside his underwear. What struck me about him was not his lowly intent, but his high intelligence. Umar Farouk Abdulmutallab was a mechanical engineer. He studied at University College London, one of the elite universities of the world. UCL accepts only supremely gifted intellects. Abdulmutallab was among the most brilliant in the world in mechanical engineering, but not bright enough to realize that if he wanted to get to Heaven and spend eternity enjoying himself with seventy-two virgins, perhaps the best course would not be to put a bomb in his underwear.

Intelligence is prone to arrogance. We can split the atom but have sown the seeds of our own destruction. We have built such sophisticated machines that we cannot turn off when they go wrong. We have so refined and computerized the accumulation of wealth that seconds of trading can bring down the world's economy. We are so smart that what took centuries to build up could be torn down in minutes.

Intelligence is fine. It is even wonderful. Smart people have facilitated human progress and have made life better. But human intelligence, such as it is today, is limited. At no time do we see the whole picture. At best, we see only a small fraction of reality.

WISDOM

Therefore, we seek not only high intelligence but vast wisdom. Wisdom is the subtle stuff of life that activates intelligence and makes it useful. It is emotional intelligence, patience, deferred gratification, ability to cope with disappointment, setbacks, loss, uncertainty, and failure. By wisdom, we mean discernment, judgment, awareness, intuition, imagination, and common sense, the capacity to integrate, to connect the dots of life. It is intelligence, but of a different type. It is social intelligence, the ability to communicate verbally and nonverbally. We might be smart; it does not mean that we will make smart decisions. Stalin was smart. Chamberlin was smart. Napoleon was smart. Putin, by all accounts, is highly intelligent. Smart people often make dumb decisions. Many smart people text and drive, never considering that it may not be a good idea to engage your handheld device while driving seventy miles an hour. Plenty of smart people never figure out that shaving or applying lipstick behind the wheel will often not end well.

The famous "marshmallow test" conducted at Stanford University established that even something as seemingly unimportant as a four-year-old's ability to defer gratification by waiting for two marshmallows, rather than grabbing one immediately, predicted better-adjusted, more popular, and higher-performing students and adults. Those four-year-old children who could not resist the temptation of one marshmallow immediately tended to be less popular, more stubborn, more compulsive, and more easily frustrated. They had a harder time dealing with stress and were reluctant to embrace new challenges. Something as basic as the ability to delay gratification as a four-year-old turned out to be an important predictor of later success.

In our workplace, would we rather have a colleague who is an untrustworthy and unreliable virtuoso, or one of average intelligence who excels in loyalty, teamwork, and discipline? Would we rather be married to a misogynist genius like Picasso, or a hard-working, loyal spouse who paints in his spare time? Who do we want running our bank? The one who was the smartest at the Wharton School, who effortlessly passed every test with flying colors, and who could devise all kinds of financial schemes that no one else could understand? Or, do we want our banker to be the one who might have been in the middle of the class but is patient, who could sit still and focus without constant need of more stimulation, more excitement, and more profit, who takes the time to analyze deeply what is presented? Who would we prefer to be with in the foxhole? The one who knows all of the theories of war, or the one who is the most resilient, the most imaginative, the most optimistic?

Therefore, wisdom is even more important to the future of the world than intelligence—and the reason that King

Solomon received a double share of it. "What is strength without a double share / Of wisdom?" wrote Milton, "Vast, unwieldy, burdensome, / Proudly secure, yet liable to fall / By weakest subtleties; not made to rule, But to subserve where wisdom bears command."

But even wisdom is not enough. There are plenty of smart people who are emotionally intelligent as well. Skillful politicians are masters of emotional intelligence. They can make you feel that you are the most important person in the room to them. They speak directly to your heart and penetrate your ego. But they often sway the masses for ill rather than good. There are all-too-many brilliant scientists who design viruses that kill. Many exceptional lawyers pervert justice. Charismatic warriors often inspire legions of followers to commit horrendous atrocities.

We can think ourselves into practically anything. We can reason ourselves into the most unreasonable positions. Most of history's evils were not accidental. They were the product of deliberation. Intelligence and wisdom can lead to catastrophe. Therefore, goodness, decency, humane values, compassion, mercy—these are the ultimate guarantor of our wellbeing, and the reason that King Solomon received more of it than any other attribute. His heart was as broad as the sands on the seashore—practically limitless.

A GOOD HEART

A good heart is the quality most prized by God, and it best advances the human condition. A good heart, not a brilliant mind, is the strongest safeguard from evil. Wicked brilliance leads to wickedness. A broad heart tempers the arrogance of our technological accomplishments and orients science toward service rather than servitude.

We do not measure moral awareness by academic excellence. We do not have to be geniuses to be ethically excellent. Moral questions do not depend on mathematical proof. We know what is right and good. We are born with moral potential, but like every other skill, moral talent must be activated. We must learn to be good. We need moral teachers. We must practice goodness. A child born with musical talent will not excel in music unless taught. Musical talent must be cultivated, honed, trained, and disciplined. A girl with athletic potential will grow up to be a champion only with training. A boy with a high IQ will excel academically only through hard work.

It is the same with moral training. Ethics, morals, generosity, compassion, kindness, forgiveness—broad heartedness—are the product of instruction, hard work, and devotion. Why do we assume that a musician must learn how to produce music but the ethical person need not learn how to produce good deeds? The athlete must train to be first in the competition, but the moral person need not train to be first in goodness? We invest a fortune to give our college-age children every opportunity to be on the dean's list but invest hardly at all for the opportunity to be on the list of the righteous of the world.

We need to practice morality, not merely think about it. We need to habituate ourselves daily to moral living and train ourselves daily for moral discipline. In the real world, it is not altruism, but duty and habit that motivate most people. The word "mitzvah" in Hebrew does not simply mean a good deed—but describes obligation, commandment, a sense of duty. We do not even have a word in Hebrew that defines charity in the manner commonly understood today. *Tsedakka* means justice—not grace. You have an obligation to support the poor. It is the law of moral behavior. Even if you do not understand it, do it anyway. Perhaps over time, you will come to understand.

Maimonides taught that it is better to give one coin to the poor on a thousand different occasions than a thousand coins all at once, because we need to train ourselves to do good. The act of giving day after day for a thousand days disciplines us to do acts of goodness. The Talmud teaches that from something that started out as having nothing to do with good intentions, through the act of doing, the intention to do good is born.

In today's America, we prioritize practical skills. We teach value, not values. We test mathematical calculus, not moral calculus. We know a lot about the cells in our body, but little about our souls. We teach young adults how to invest money, not how to give money. So many Americans have never been so educated and so ignorant about what is truly important. We are obsessed with celebrity and are strangely apathetic to suffering. We follow the exploits of fallen athletes, politicians, and actors twenty-four hours a day, but care nothing about the downfall of Man; the thousands who will die today from malnutrition or easily preventable diseases; the millions in our country who are jobless, prospectless, and helpless.

Every day we suffer the consequences. We pay the price in broken homes, broken marriages, and broken lives. Many might have affluence and professional status, but they are not happy or fulfilled. The cream of American society, feasting on the fat of the land, is spiritually starving.

We will not overcome the great challenges of society through science and technology alone. We will not manifest the best of ourselves through intelligence and wisdom alone. We must also learn broad-heartedness and train others in it. Our highest humanity always leads to someone or something other than ourselves. "The beginning and the end of Torah are acts of kindness," the sages teach. The more we actualize our humanity, the more we act to serve others, help others, love others, and believe in others. Our most inspirational moments are when we peer into our own nature, intuiting the moral sentiment that lies at the core of the human creature.

I met Alessio in Krakow, an Italian chef who felt that he could not stand idly by and watch the suffering inflicted on Ukrainians. On his own, and using his own money, he began cooking for refugees, in train stations, hospitals, and at the border. Every few weeks, he would make the dangerous trek into Ukraine and offer meals. He spoke of desperately hungry people fighting for food. It reminded me of the stories I heard of fights amongst prisoners in concentration camps for small morsels of bread. When I met Alessio, he estimated that he had already cooked and served 40,000 meals. People who heard of his exceptional generosity and courage contributed resources to him so that he could continue cooking.

I encountered dozens of other humanitarian aid workers in Poland. People who dropped everything in their home countries to encamp on the Ukrainian border, and in Polish cities and towns, motivated by the desire to do good and driven by the impulse of compassion and kindness. We never have enough of such people. "There is always more misery in the depths than compassion in the heights," wrote Victor Hugo.

I have no idea how intelligent these humanitarians are. I do not know whether they are especially wise. But I do know that they are the best of us. They have the broadest heart, a heart as vast as the sands on the seashore.

It is upon these people that the future wellbeing of the world rests.

Afterword

One who teaches Torah to the child of another,
it is as if he formed that student.

(Babylonian Talmud Sanhedrin 99b)

The Babylonian Talmud begins on page two. The first page is blank—symbolizing that we never begin at the beginning. Something always preceded what is. Everything is a product of what came before. Nothing just materializes. The Torah, itself, starts with the second letter of the Hebrew alphabet, not the first. Jewish commentators emphasized that "In the Beginning" does not literally mean creation out of nothing. God created many worlds before settling on this one.

Since there is no beginning, there can be no end. As soon as Jews complete reading the last word of Deuteronomy in the annual Torah cycle, without even taking a breath, we begin anew, with the first words of Genesis. "There is no before and no after in the Torah," the commentator Rashi asserted. Judaism is one constant flow, fed by endless tributaries and streams that forever nourish the wellsprings of Jewish existence. When we engage Judaism, we join the flow. The chronological time and place of our participation is not decisive. What matters is that we are inside the never-ending current of Jewish life, mixing with all who came before and all who will follow, keeping the eternal waters of Torah churning. The constant swirl ensures that the waters never stagnate. They are always fresh.

Hence, an afterword is never the last word. There will always be a word after this word. The highest achievement in Judaism is that the seeds we planted in our times bear fruit in future times.

The Talmud describes Honi, the righteous, who once saw a man by the side of the road planting a carob tree. Honi asked the man, "How long does it take for this tree to bear fruit?" The man replied, "Seventy years." Honi then asked, are you certain that you will live for another seventy years?" The man replied, "I found carob trees in the world; as my ancestors planted them for me, so, I too, plant these for my children."

I write these words in 2022. Seventy years from now, I will have long gone to my eternal reward. I address these last thoughts to the Jews of 2092, most of whose parents are not yet born. As my ancestors implanted them in me, so I pass them on to you, testimonials of the dreams of our generation. I pray that in this way, we will meet by the Tree of Jewish Life in the Garden of Eternity:

Dear Jews of the Future,

Peace and blessings upon you. I reach out to you from the past in love and devotion. The first thing I want to say is I am relieved that you are there to read this. Many in our generation doubted that. We were quite lost in 2022. We were losing more American Jews that those being born. The liberal Jewish movements, especially, were hemorrhaging. Less than half of Reform Jews said that being Jewish was very important to them. We were producing 1.7 children per family unit, way below the replacement level, and fewer than half of these children were enrolled in formal Jewish education.

It was a challenging time to be a rabbi. We, who devoted our lives to the invigoration and continuation of the Jewish people, were presiding over what many felt was the disintegration of American Judaism. In our most despondent moods, we felt as if we were living the last days of Pompeii, our people blissfully unaware of the looming catastrophe. Many professional observers were so distressed that they predicted you would never materialize: that you would be something else—the Jewish component of your family having long ago blown away on the crosscurrents of complacency.

So if you are reading this, you should realize how remarkable it is that you are still Jewish. In a sense, you are the remnant of American Jews, those who made it through the 21st century. You made it because someone in your family that I may have known as a child was determined to carry on. Though we will never meet, I feel an inexplicable kinship with you. I became a rabbi because of you. If I knew for sure that it would all end with me, what would have been the point of devoting my life to this endeavor? The purpose of devotion is to inspire others to continue the journey. You are alive; and because you are alive, we, too, are still alive, in your thoughts and in your deeds. Because you are alive, our lives had meaning. You grant us the gift of retroactive merit. We did our job. We built the bridge to you.

That you are there to read this leads me to assume that you have the essential element of the Jewish personality that sustained our people from the beginning:

Hope.

Judaism is hope. Hope that tomorrow will be better than today; hope that we will endure, no matter what: That we are an eternal people, and that our very existence testifies to the existence of God. Never lose hope for the next generation. Keep building: Build for yourselves, your children, their children, and other people's children.

No matter what your surveys predict about the future of the Jewish community—and remember—our surveys predicted that you would not exist—keep assuming that there will be Jews in America in the 22nd century, and that you are responsible for them. They will not exist if you will not be devoted to them. They will not appear if you do not appear interested in them. Keep nudging, cajoling, and demanding that the generation of your day support the generation of the next day. All of Judaism is based on this. We found centers of Jewish life and learning in our world. As our ancestors built them for us, we, too, build centers of Judaism for our children. In this way the chain of Jewish transmission is sustained. One generation builds for another. One generation plants for another.

We did many things well in our generation. We were at the pinnacle of accomplishment and achievement. Jews were among the most affluent and the most educated of all Americans. We built sparkling centers of Jewish life and generously supported practically every major cultural institution of this country. It seemed that wherever there was something important going on, Jews were part of it. Jewish contributions to civic life were everywhere. A ten-block walk in any neighborhood of Manhattan revealed the extent of Jewish involvement. You could see it on the walls and in the literature of hospitals, museums, schools, cultural centers, and universities. Jews even helped sustain New York City churches. Jewish scholarship was better in our day than any other day. More Jewish books were published; more university classes were offered; and more non-Jews were interested in, studied, and chose Judaism than ever before.

Alas, it wasn't enough. Nothing was enough. Something fundamental was missing and we couldn't figure it out. But you already know that, because it is seventy years from now and you know how the last seven decades unfolded.

We tried hard. We produced learned papers; we had regular conferences. We spoke about Jewish continuity constantly. Our people grew weary of our prophecies of doom, and many simply tuned us out. But those who ignored the looming catastrophe only exacerbated the trends. Those who did not speak about raising a Jewish family and investing in Jewish children conveyed the message that Judaism has nothing to do with the collective future of the Jewish people: there is no Jewish distinctiveness, no boundaries, no demands, and no obligations. Nothing asked; nothing given; nothing done: so typical of our generation of Americans.

I don't write this to excuse us from what may be your harsh judgment, simply to explain that we were aware of the problem but couldn't figure out how to reverse the trends. There are no excuses. History does not accept excuses. While on a personal level, trying hard is often enough, and in any case, what more can one person do but his very best—from the perspective of history, the test is not whether you have done your best. History demands results. History requires success. To fail in history is to disappear. One cursory glance at the annals of old uncovers cemeteries of sleeping civilizations—graveyards of ancient cultures—that tried their best but lie unremembered and unsung in unvisited tombs. If the carob tree does not bear fruit in seventy years, does it matter that the farmer tried his best? All that history cares about is that there is no tree of life. It didn't survive, either because it was not sufficiently cultivated or because the soil itself was hostile to its survival.

My dear descendants: to be alive on the cusp of the 22nd century; what a gift! Your time has come. The entire past and future of our people are in your hands. Our mistakes—as our accomplishments—are not your destiny. This is one of the axiomatic principles of Judaism. You can figure out what we could not. Perhaps you already have: an exhilarating thought that gives relief to this worried wonderer.

May you enjoy the many gifts we have bequeathed to you, and may you forgive our many faults. It is the Jewish way to look back at past generations with gratitude for their successes and a kinder judgment of their failures, a verdict softened by the transition of time.

May you live long lives, of worth and productivity, contributing to the vitality of the Jewish people and to the good of all people. Plant the saplings now, as your ancestors did before you, and they will bear fruit in three generations.

I bless you from ages past.

P.S.: If I am wrong, and there is no American Jewish afterword, may these words be placed in the museum of the history of American Judaism as a testimonial to what might have been.

P.P.S: I am not wrong.

Rabbi Ammiel Hirsch